START AND RUN A

Fish and Chip Shop
or Burger Bar

Visit our How To website at www.howto.co.uk

At www.howto.co.uk you can engage in conversation with our authors – all of whom have 'been there and done that' in their specialist fields. You can get access to special offers and additional content but most importantly you will be able to engage with, and become a part of, a wide and growing community of people just like yourself.

At www.howto.co.uk you'll be able to talk and share tips with people who have similar interests and are facing similar challenges in their lives. People who, just like you, have the desire to change their lives for the better – be it through moving to a new country, starting a new business, growing their own vegetables, or writing a novel.

At www.howto.co.uk you'll find the support and encouragement you need to help make your aspirations a reality.

For more information on starting and running your own fish and chip shop or burger bar visit www.startandrunachipshoporburgerbar.co.uk

How To Books strives to present authentic, inspiring, practical infomation in their books. Now, when you buy a title from **How To Books**, you get even more than just words on a page.

START AND RUN A

Fish and Chip Shop or Burger Bar

James Kayui Li

howtobooks / **smallbusinessstart-ups**

Published by How To Books Ltd,
Spring Hill House, Spring Hill Road,
Begbroke, Oxford OX5 1RX, United Kingdom
Tel: (01865) 375794, Fax: (01865) 379162
info@howtobooks.co.uk
www.howtobooks.co.uk

British Library Cataloguing in Publication Data
A catalogue record for this book is available from the British Library

ISBN: 978 1 84528 308 7

Cover design by Baseline Arts Ltd, Oxford
Produced for How To Books by Deer Park Productions, Tavistock
Typeset by Pantek Arts Ltd, Maidstone, Kent.
Printed and bound in Great Britain by Cromwell Press Group Ltd, Trowbridge, Wiltshire

I dedicate this book to my daughter Angela

CONTENTS

INTRODUCTION

Running a small catering business like a fish and chip shop/burger bar business is challenging. It involves preparing and selling food, managing staff well and providing a high standard of service.

I began working for my mother in her fast food outlet in my teens and I now own and run my own business. In *How to start and run your own Fish and Chip Shop or Burger Bar* I will share my experiences of the trade – after you have read this book you will know a lot about this business and should know how to make good fish and chips!

Perhaps you are bored with your current job, or you want to open up your own business in a holiday resort, or you would like to be your own boss. Maybe you just love fish and chips, beef burgers and fast food in general and would like to prepare and sell them for a living. The fish bar and takeaway business is like being in any other business: you must be committed and, above all, enjoy what you're doing. Of course, you must like and believe in your product. I love to eat fish and chips and am a fan of fast food. Nothing tastes quite like fresh fish and chips with salt and vinegar. Yummy! I also frequently indulge in burgers topped with salad and cheese or fried chicken pieces.

How to start and run your own Fish and Chip Shop or Burger Bar will benefit people already in the trade, and certainly help people who are interested in it. If eating fast foods is a passion of yours and if it is what you want to do as a career, then this book is for you.

1

THE ORIGINS OF FISH AND CHIPS AND BEEF BURGERS

Let's start by looking at how the two fast foods actually started – how they began, developed and embedded themselves into the culture of their home country. How, through time, the popularity of both foods meant that they became part of the food culture in other places of the world.

Where did fish and chips come from?

The fact is nobody really knows where fish and chips came from. What we do know for sure was that fish and chips were invented separately. The potato was believed to have been brought to Europe by Sir Walter Raleigh back in the 17th century, and the French thought of cutting potatoes into chips, called *pommes de terre à la mode*. In 2004, a professor at the University of De Montfort in Leicester carried out a research project on the global influence of British food and he claimed that fish and chips was probably a combination of *pomme frites* and a fish dish influenced by the Jewish culture. Although the origin of the meal is complex, the project suggests it was probably brought to the UK by immigrants in the 19th century. The combination of fried fish and chips appeared in the Victorian era and has become very much a part of British culture and tradition as fish and chip shops opened here as early as the 1860s.

The first fish and chip shops

A Jewish immigrant, Joseph Malin from Eastern Europe, is said to have opened the first fish and chip shop in the east end of London in 1860 and John Lees opened his business a few years later, setting up a wooden hut in the market at Mossley, near Oldham in Lancashire. He moved to another premises later where he placed a notice on his window claiming his business was 'The first fish and chip shop in the world'. Apparently, his two grandsons are also currently in the fish and chip shop business and seem to enjoy being in the industry that their grandfather had a great influence in starting. The first mention of fish being fried was in Charles Dickens's *Oliver Twist* published in 1838, where there is reference to a 'fried fish warehouse'. So perhaps they had appeared even earlier.

During the industrial revolution fleets and icing equipment were developed which allowed cheaper supplies of sea fish. Railways were established and helped the distribution of fish to every part of the country. Fish that landed at a port in Grimsby could be expected to be on sale in the distant parts of the UK early the next morning. Also the income of the working class had risen so they had a little spare cash for buying fish and chips. By 1910 there were around 25,000 fish and chip shops in Britain. At the peak in 1927 there were 35,000, with two thirds of the white fish caught being deep fat fried.

The fish and chip shop had become a typical family business and even to this day it tends to be a family-oriented business run by husband and wife. The trade would be carried on from people's front rooms (a practice hardly likely to be approved by today's hygiene standards!). Practically every working community had at least one chip shop, fuelling factory workers and other shift workers through the working day. People would also make fishcakes by mixing left over bits of fish with mashed potato, and they are still being served today.

As well as cod, other types of white fish were used – in Yorkshire it had to be haddock (very similar to cod) and Lancashire preferred hake. In the northeast people liked to use rock salmon and dogfish. Unfortunately, however, early fish and chip shops had only very basic cooking facilities which consisted of a large cauldron of cooking fat that was heated by a coal fire. An unpleasant smell was produced from frying which led authorities to classify the business as an 'offensive trade', but it bounced back from this reputation during the Second World War when food supplies were scarce. The government rationed certain foods such as meat, eggs and milk, but fish and chips were not subject to rationing. The cuisine fed the masses through war times and it was the main takeaway food, as it was fish and chips or nothing.

Why is this tradition still popular today?

Simply because it is delicious, and also beneficial to the body because fish and chips are made from natural ingredients. Fresh fish is used and chips are made from fresh potatoes. Fish and chips are unlike other fast foods which will usually be processed and stored frozen. Perhaps it is also the distinct aroma and taste along with its inexpensive price tag. It is eaten by every generation; the older generation saw the early days of the dish when it had little to no competition, and they remember when it used to be wrapped in newspaper.

An older generation introduces fish and chips to a younger generation and they in turn introduce it to a generation younger than them. Its diversity as a food eaten by all age groups is unmatched by any fast food. It is a symbol of British heritage and having fried fish and chips together can make the perfect lunch or dinner.

Often when people visit their local Chinese takeaway they order fish and chips to accompany their meal. The demand and popularity of fish and chips has even influenced many restaurants to include it on their menus. The national dish, sometimes referred to as a national treasure, will continue being appreciated by every generation.

Nourishing and low in fat

A portion of fish and chips contains vitamins, protein, fibre and iron. Even today if you ask most people whether they think fish and chips are good value for money in comparison with other fast foods, many would say yes. Fish and Chips also contain less fat than its rivals; on average there is 9.42 grammes of fat per 100 grammes, beating other takeaway food. The average pizza has 11 grammes, a beef burger and fries has around 12.5 grammes and kebab has as much as 16 grammes. There is also more fat in a chicken tikka masala and a portion of fried rice. So not only is fish and chips good value and nutritious, eaten infrequently it could even be suitable for weight watching. Chips also absorb less fat than thinner-sized 'French fries'. Eating fish has always been widely recommended and is thought to be beneficial to the brain.

Research carried out in 2007 by food intolerance experts, yorktest.com, put the potato as the number one safest food to eat in Britain. A list of the safest foods was compiled – foods least likely to provoke an allergy – and the potato came out on top. With all its nutritional qualities, goodness and flavour, the food is least likely to have links with migraine, eczema or fatigue.

Facts and figures

The most successful fish and chip shop owner was Harry Ramsden (1888-1963). In 1928 he started trading in a wooden hut at Guiseley, close to Leeds. He set the world record at 10,000 fish and chip meals sold in one day in 1952. Today *Harry Ramsden* is a worldwide restaurant chain and the record has been broken three more times – it currently stands at 12,105. Harry Ramsden's is also famous for the Harry Ramsden Challenge where customers have to finish a giant piece of cod, large chips and peas which gains them a certificate and sometimes a complimentary dessert.

In 2001, the then-prime minister Tony Blair chose to do a photo shoot in a fish and chip shop in Yorkshire during his election campaign. This delicious meal represents British identity as much as Shakespeare and Big Ben in London. The British consumed nearly 300 million servings of this dish in 1999 and on average over 255 million fish and chip meals are sold every single year. That's a lot of fish and chips. A survey found that 30 per cent of people miss their fish and chips when they are abroad on holiday. Even celebrity chef Rick Stein couldn't resist opening his own restaurant in Padstow in Cornwall – called 'Stein's Fish and Chips'.

> In the UK, on Fridays, 20 per cent of meals brought into the home are from fish and chip shops.

The world's biggest ever portion of fish and chips was fried in Hull, in October 2002. The giant fillet measured 34 inches long and 14 inches wide, weighing 28 pounds and 1 ounce, beating the previous world record by two pounds.

National Chip Week takes place every year in February and is organised by the Potato Council which celebrates 'the chip' by promoting it through fish and chip shops. A Valentine's theme is added by calling them 'love chips'. People can nominate a food premises such as a pub or restaurant that makes the best chips, and the winners are determined by votes and a decision from the Potato Council. Nominees that win receive a prestigious National Chip Award. On the website www.lovechips.co.uk there are facts about the history of chips, a fun and games section, as well as chip recipes.

The representative body of fish and chips is the National Federation of Fish Friers, set up in 1913. It represents, promotes and protects the interests of fish and chip shop owners throughout the UK. They work with Seafish, an authority which works to promote the quality of sustainable seafood in the UK. Their monthly trade magazine sent to members has information related to the industry and contains tips to decrease running costs and increase sales. Non-members can subscribe for a fee without having to join as a member. For more information go their website at www.federationoffishfriers.co.uk

A contest is held annually for the title of 'Fish and Chip Shop of the Year' that aims to find the best-produced portion of fish and chips (with first place, runners up and regional winners). Another contest held is for 'Young Fish Frier of the Year' which young people in the industry can enter.

Fry, a monthly magazine created for the fish frying and fast food industry, offers the latest industry news, promotes products and interviews influential people in the trade. It also covers a day with a fish and chip shop owner in which they are able to give advice on business. They have a very comprehensive website (www.fry-online.co.uk) which aims to combine everything related to the industry and concentrates on improving the fish and chip business.

Fish & Chips and Fast Food is another magazine dedicated to the industry and fast food in general. It is distributed free to outlets and claims to have reached nearly every small fast-food business in the UK. It also offers news in the industry, case studies and lots of product advertisements that support existing fast-food businesses.

Worldwide fish and chips phenomenon?

After almost 150 years of service fish and chips continues to be popular and it has even spread to the Mediterranean coast of Spain, overseas holiday resorts, America, Canada and Australia. Even punters at Las Vegas can order the dish between placing their bets. The dish has been found in the strangest places – on top of cliffs in South Africa and even in a desert in Oman. Fish and chips has also started to appear in China, a country that has a large diverse range of traditional cuisine. The first fish and chip shop in China opened its doors for business in 2004 in Beijing. The shop, named 'Fish Nation', serves thick hand-cut chips and cod, fried in beer batter. The dish has been well received by modern Beijingers and the owners have expanded their business by opening further outlets.

I am sure that fish and chips will continue to appear in many parts of the world making a positive impact with other food cultures. The reason for its popularity could be the golden brown appearance or its aroma when sprinkled with salt and vinegar. Or perhaps it's the interesting history behind it. Whatever the reason, this traditional British cuisine will continue to be famous around the globe offering high nutritional value and, most of all, to be liked by our taste buds.

The beginnings of the beef burger

You may be surprised, but the origin of beef burgers is even more uncertain than fish and chips. People think that the nation's barbecue favourite was an American invention and they might be right. But there are multiple claims as to where this world-recognised food actually began.

Burgers are usually fried or grilled and are a patty of ground beef served in a bun with salad. A slice of cheese is often placed on a burger to make it a cheeseburger. Beef burgers have also been commonly referred to as a hamburgers which is the one and the same, and is not normally made from pork. The name of hamburger is in fact believed to have come from Hamburg in Germany. People there ate meat scraps, which were similar to ground beef and served with a piece of round bread. It has been claimed that German immigrants took this style of eating to the United States, which the Americans loved and developed into an international food favourite.

A different story of origin again comes from the German city of Hamburg, where a restaurant cook named Otto Kuasw made hamburgers in 1891. This was a ground beef sausage fried in batter and sandwiched between two slices of buttered bread, along with a fried egg. This sandwich, known as Deutsches beefsteak, was a popular snack for sailors who stopped at the Hamburg port. It is said that the sailors brought tales of this meal to America in 1894 when they visited the port of New York.

Another story is that a man called Oscar Webe Bilby built an iron grill at his home in Bowden, Oklahoma. He shaped some Angus meat into round patties and fried them on the grill, and served them to his friends along with freshly-made ice cream and root beer. The meal was so popular that it became an annual event, sometimes bringing in a crowd of 125 people.

There is also evidence from the Menches Brothers. In 1885 the two brothers were selling their pork patty sandwiches at the Erie County fair in Hamburg, New York and ran out of pork. Unable to get more of the meat from their suppliers, they used beef instead. They added coffee, brown sugar and other flavours to the meat and called their invention the Hamburg Sandwich, which evolved later on to being called hamburger.

The state of Wisconsin, US, also makes a claim as the birthplace of the burger. In 1885, at the age of 15, Charles Nagreen started a meatball business at the Outagamie County fair. His business was unsuccessful as meatballs were not very convenient to eat, so he decided to flatten the meatballs and place them between two slices of bread. His business took off and he continued trading until his death in 1951.

Today Wisconsin holds an annual burger festival in August, and hosts the world's largest hamburger parade! A 8,266 pound hamburger was cooked on the mammoth 'Charlie Grill' on 4 August 2001. Another claim is from Louis Lassen of New Haven, Connecticut. In 1890 he served the first 'burger' at his New Haven luncheonette, Louis' Lunch. He ground up some beef, then served it in the form of a sandwich to a customer who had to eat on the run.

A popular story of the origins of the hamburger is from the St Louis World Fair in 1904. Many Texans believe that the credit for the first hamburger goes to Fletcher 'Old Dave' Davis from Athens in Texas. He took a raw hamburger steak and grilled it to a crisp brown, then sandwiched it between two thick slices of home-made toast with a large slice of raw onion. His sandwich was popular and inspired Old Dave to open a hamburger stand at The Pike, at the St Louis World Fair Louisiana Purchase Exhibition.

He has also been credited as the creator of French fries, selling fried potato strips with his hamburgers at the world fair. The idea was said to have been given to him by a friend in Paris, Texas. Unfortunately, the reporter covering the story mistook Paris as the capital city of France and as a result potato strips were known as 'French' fries.

Despite the success of the beef burger in the US it was first looked down on by the majority of Americans as a low grade meat that would cause food poisoning. Another concern was that people frequently thought that the meat came from slaughterhouse scraps. Things started to turn around in 1921 with the birth of the first White Castle Hamburger joint in Wichita, Kansas. It was a business venture between Edgar Waldo 'Billy' Ingram and hamburger bun inventor J Walter Anderson. They promoted the idea that hamburger meat was both clean and safe by moving the kitchen from the back of the shop to the front so that customers could see how fresh the raw beef was. They had fresh meat delivered twice a day and an experiment was carried out to prove that a hamburger had nutritional value. To develop the business they placed coupons in daily newspapers and sold hamburgers for five cents each. Later, they discovered that putting holes in the burgers helped the beef cook more evenly, and that was how White Castle beef burgers came to have five holes. Ingram patented this, as well as the first fast food paper hat.

White Castle imitators later began introducing variations to the hamburger, including Bob's Big Boy double patty burger. The cheeseburger was invented by Lionel Clark Stenberger in 1924 when he tried placing a layer of cheese in a hamburger at his father's short-order shop in Pasadena, California. However, there have been also other claims to the cheeseburger invention. By the 1940s and 1950s, the appearance of cars created the trend of drive-through restaurants as hamburgers were delivered to the automobiles by young women on roller-skates. Not long after this, the two major hamburger restaurant chains Burger King and McDonald's had begun, which both started as small outlets. Like American movies, the beef burger spread its influence to the rest of the world and its popularity grew. Some regard the beef burger as one of the best ideas in history.

Burgers Today

The US consumes the most beef burgers – 25 billion of them are eaten there every year. They have many versions of the burger as different toppings are used and the way it is served is different by region. The most famous beef burger is the 'Big Mac' from fast food giant McDonald's. The company operates its 30,000 restaurants in over 120 countries around the world, and you are very likely to come across a McDonald's in any major city. Through their rigorous and clever marketing and effective business systems they have become the dominant fast-food retailer and are truly global (although they actually appeared in the UK relatively late – in the 1970s – as branches opened in other parts of Europe first). Since their arrival, they have become a major part of British fast-food culture and continue to be popular.

Beef burgers are a favourite snack after visiting a bar or nightclub. Statistics released by Keep Britain Tidy show that beef burgers and kebabs are the most popular food choices after a night on the town. Perhaps it is because they are not difficult to carry and are suited to almost everybody's taste.

The enormous international appeal of burgers is a true phenomenon and they are widely eaten in households as well as being a popular takeaway – families often have burger and chips for dinner. Some people like to make their own burgers from fresh, by using minced beef and adding their own herbs and flavours. The combination of beef, bread and fresh salad topped with sauce never fails to please.

The demand and statistics of fast food

In 2005 the fast food and takeaway market in the UK was valued at £8.38 billion by Key Note Consultancy. The UK is the largest fast-food and take-away market in Europe, twice the size of Germany and three times the size of the French market. The burger sector was worth £1.86b and fish and chips was worth £939 million in 2004.

In 2005, research by Euromonitor International, a consumer food service, found that fast food was booming. According to their research, quality was a main factor in the growth of fast food. One of their senior research analysts commented that, 'Fast food in the UK has improved in quality in most sectors to such an extent that it is now often equal to what one would find in a full service restaurant'.

There have been many claims that consuming fast foods has strong links with obesity. In the United States – the home of fast food – one in three people is obese. Some claim that the reasons are more to do with lack of exercise and self discipline – fast food may be a factor in causing weight issues, but many people today are inactive and over-indulge when eating any form of food. There are other claims that many people's work consists of desk jobs that involve little or no physical exercise. Technology also plays a strong part, as more people are sitting in front of computer screens and watching television excessively. Playing computer games is also a popular activity with young people as well as adults. Even the use of cars has been brought into the debate, as people walk less. Looking at these other factors, fast food outlets cannot possibly take all the responsibility for people who suffer from weight problems.

The future for fast foods

Quickly-prepared food will carry on being a part of people's budgets. It is easily available and reasonably inexpensive, and many people do not want to cook seven days a week. The food is bought in and there is no time needed for its preparation – even convenience meals from supermarkets have to be prepared using a microwave. There are no dishes to wash and the packaging can be placed in the bin. These meals can also provide nutritional content. In fact all fast foods, eaten with some salad or vegetables, can be of benefit to the body and some can closely substitute the nutritional value of a proper home-cooked meal. With the population increasing and the quality and standards of fast food improving, the market is likely to continue to be strong.

Summary

In this chapter we have covered the early history of fish and chips, and the story of the beefburger. As you now know the beginnings of these foods, you should have a deeper understanding of them. It is important to have more knowledge of what you sell. The chapter has also made you aware of the present activities of the two food types. Having looked at the statistics of people consuming fast food in this country, it is clear there is a high demand for fast food and a main reason is its convenience. Based on the history of fish and chips and beef burgers, and the number of people who buy them, it is safe to predict there will always be a demand for them.

2
STARTING IN THE BUSINESS

It's important to be aware of the realities of going into any business, and to decide if this type of business is suited to you.

The realities of being in business

With today's business world being more and more competitive, it can be a difficult road to follow. You might have to be brave and give up the security of your current employment – business can be unpredictable and affected by competition. There are, of course, rewards in being your own boss – the possible financial rewards, and being an employer of people rather than an employee. However, most businesses can run well only with the support of staff and you will have to train and supervise them. In this business, they're only as good as what you can teach them.

The point is that going into business for yourself is no joke. If you're willing to work at it, you can reap the financial rewards; if not, you could end up in financial disaster! There will be utility bills to pay, monthly bank loan payments (I assume you may need to borrow some money from a bank) as well as business rates and council tax. You will also have to pay the expenses for your own home.

 If you have always been an employee and you're fed up working for someone else, don't be fooled that it will be any easier working for yourself.

There are some luxuries that you don't have to think about as an employee:

☐ You don't have to worry about the business or company you work for as you still receive your monthly pay.

☐ You don't have to pay staff or running costs.

☐ You don't have to sacrifice time that could be spent with your family, friends or doing other activities.

□ You don't have the burden of greater responsibilities to your bank, the council, suppliers and of course your customers.

□ You don't have to worry about paying the bills even if the business is not doing as well as it should.

□ You aren't stuck in your business – you have fewer responsibilities and the power to walk away from your job at any time. In business you simply cannot, and if you decide to sell up it can take some time for the business to sell; you could be waiting a few years or more before you can move on.

If you run your business and you have children, you will lose time with them. Most of your time will be spent running and improving the business operation. You will of course have to give up some time with your partner or spouse too unless you're both involved in the running of the business.

I must mention that going into business with a spouse can be a difficult ordeal if you have never before worked together. There can be disagreements and arguments which may have negative effects on the relationship. Such a change can put a strain on your seemingly healthy relationship and will no doubt have an effect on any children you have. To put in plainly, business is tough. Without the right preparation, know-how and correct management, its chances of success are greatly hindered.

Why some businesses fail

New businesses start up every year, but many of them do not succeed. This section explores reasons why this happens.

AN INADEQUATE BUSINESS PLAN

Many small businesses fail because of lack of planning. Your plan needs to be realistic and you need ideas and strategies to have a blueprint for success. A weak business plan may not support the future challenges you will face in business.

CASH FLOW PROBLEMS

A common mistake for many failed businesses is having insufficient operating funds. People underestimate how much money is needed when operating a business. They may also have unrealistic expectations of business turnover. As the business operates and grows you have to budget realistically and not use the income from the business on personal spending. Although banks can offer a solution to ease cash flow problems in the form of an overdraft, that may lead to more problems. The costs of an overdraft facility, especially when over its limit, are very high.

EXPANDING TOO QUICKLY

It can be tempting to rush to expand and over-forecast the business without properly establishing it, which leads to serious problems. The business needs time to get a strong foundation.

POOR LOCATION

This is a common reason for failure. It does not matter how well you manage your premises – the wrong area or neighbourhood is a perfect recipe for failure. The location needs to be given a lot of thought to assess its suitability for business. (There is guidance on this in chapter 3.)

POOR MANAGEMENT AND LEADERSHIP SKILLS

Some regard this as the number one reason for business failures. Novice first-time employers are likely to be missing strong business management skills and their lack of expertise in finance, production, and managing employees can affect their operation. Businesses need to be properly managed so that every part of the operation can function well. A crucial part is the hiring and correct leadership of employees and the constant improvement of the business operation.

COMPETITION

This affects businesses of all types. New businesses need to know who their competitors are, and decide whether they can give people a better product or service.

PARTNERSHIP ISSUES

When in business with a spouse or partner, issues may arise. Within a general partnership each partner is individually liable for the business activities of the other. If a partner leaves without any notice, the remaining partner is liable for all the debts. There could be disagreements relating to falling out, or when one partner no longer wants to be in the business. There is no total control over the business by any single person. The decision-making process is shared and can lead to disagreements. All these issues within a partnership can affect the progress of the business and may lead to its failure.

HAVING NO UNIQUE SELLING POINT

Being too similar to your competitors in terms of product or service will put the business at a disadvantage. Food business owners should be creative so that their premises carry its own personality or individuality. There could be more product choice on the menu, a modern fitted premises or just overall better service. A food business should try to be different from similar businesses in order to stand out from the competition.

POOR CUSTOMER SERVICE AND EMPLOYEE INCOMPETENCE

Staff that are poorly trained have many negative effects. They represent part of the business, and as a result their mistakes in service, and how they treat customers, will affect its growth. When staff do most of the serving the owners are not as close to the customer. The employees need to be able to perform to a high level and have strong customer service skills to generate repeat business. This is a crucial point for long-term success.

INEFFECTIVE ADVERTISING

The business needs to be promoted so that people know that the service exists. Marketing the business gives it more chances for growth and encourages new business to come through the door. Without advertising, the business may not be able to get more market share and turnover will be very difficult to increase. Successful businesses, no matter what size, regularly have advertising campaigns; they usually find what forms of advertising work. Not all forms of advertising are suited to small food businesses. Marketing your business using the wrong methods will waste capital and do nothing for the business.

TREATING IT AS A HOBBY

Sometimes people start a business because it is something they like doing. If you like cooking it does not necessarily mean you will be good at running a restaurant or food outlet. In the food business you need to be competent in all areas – not just the cooking.

LACK OF COMMITMENT

One thing that should never be in short supply is commitment. If you are not going to give 100 per cent or more of yourself when running a business, then don't bother – it will save you a lot of headaches. You need to do your homework and have done the appropriate preparation before going into your new business venture, but it is only long-term commitment that will make you resistant to the pressures and challenges of it. You can't ever make something successful by cutting corners, especially in the competitive world of business. As they say, you get back only what you put in. You will have to plan everything carefully and be ready to do a lot of hard work.

With some hard work and perseverance, being in business can be a profitable and enjoyable experience.

Despite all these problems, starting a business can also be a brave and worthwhile ambition. And if you are committed enough and prepared enough beforehand, then becoming self-employed could be a start of a bright future. I am certain it will make you grow as a person and give you valuable experience which you may not be able to get when you're an employee.

Is this the right business for you?

DO YOU LIKE TO BE ACTIVE?

In this business you won't be sitting around – the job requires you to be reasonably fit. If you are somewhat overweight then you might want to consider getting fitter before running a business like this. Even if you aim to employ staff to do most of the work it's a good idea to get fit anyway because the challenges of this trade will be more manageable.

DO YOU LIKE TALKING TO PEOPLE?

If your current job is in sales, for example, and you like meeting people and having a chat, then it will help in this sort of catering where you will have a lot of contact with customers. Bear in mind that you may have to do all this talking while cooking and preparing food, which is a bit tricky. Just as hairdressers keep their customers amused when working on their hair, talking to customers will allow you to get to know them which can help in encouraging them to return.

I have two middle-aged ladies who sometimes come in as often as three times a week. They're very friendly and chatty so they feel more like friends than just customers. Building a relationship with your customers is essential to sustain business and long-term growth. You have to try to create goodwill so that people will use your shop instead of another. Good communication is essential to win customers

CAN YOU CREATE A POSITIVE IMAGE?

You must leave customers with a positive image of your business as you're trying to establish yourself. Even if you have taken over from an already successful business, it is you who are now running it so there is work to be done to maintain the turnover. I have seen people invest in successful food businesses only to find that six months later their turnover has decreased.

Unfortunately we are creatures of habit and it is true that customers do not like change. When they notice a change in the standard of service, some customers will not return. People can also grow fond of the previous owners, so the only way to draw them in is by the quality you provide in your service and by building a rapport with them. An owner who is miserable can break the business and there have been shops that have been transformed when taken over by the right person.

CAN YOU KEEP A SMILE ON YOUR FACE, EVEN WHEN YOU DON'T WANT TO?

The product is food, but customer service is also very important. Of course the quality of the food is a major part in the success of your business, but you must also try to be a friendly person and appear happy when people enter your shop. You have only one chance to make a good first impression. Customers keep the business running and without them the business will not exist.

DO YOU MIND GETTING YOUR HANDS DIRTY?

You will definitely be doing a lot of frying. Your hands will be in contact with raw meat, and fish batter will stick to them. Running a catering outlet is not a paper-based job although there is a paperwork side to any business. The work is hands-on with food preparation and cleaning duties.

CAN YOU GET USED TO THE HOURS?

It is not a nine-to-five job. You may finish late in the evening (depending on your particular shop). You may have to work on Saturdays so if you have children then your time with them during these hours will be sacrificed. If you are going into this trade with your partner, and plan to employ staff, then perhaps one of you can take a night off to spend time with the kids.

HAVE YOU GOT THE ENERGY?

A catering business is not quite the same as other retail businesses. I have a friend who runs her own card shop which sells other items such as party accessories. She has a lot of work, including making attractive displays inside the shop, but everything is pretty much ready for sale once a customer walks in. It is not the same in food businesses – once a customer arrives and orders what they want you need to cook it before a sale is made. So there is a physical demand as you're on your feet and working up a sweat.

You have to be alert when an order is received and react fast to get preparing and cooking. There are stresses and pressures like monitoring the turnover every week and maintaining and improving the quality of service. Your business will need to generate enough income to keep up loan and bill payments, including staff wages, and to make a profit for yourself. The unusual working hours will also be very unsociable.

Testing the water

If you have already had a taste of what it is like working in a fast food environment, feel free to skip through this part. If you have not worked in fast food, it's a good idea to get a part-time job working in one. You could ask at a local shop or perhaps you know a friend or relative who owns an outlet. Or maybe you know someone who has past work experience in a similar business and could offer some advice. I recommend you test it out to see if you enjoy the work because when you own one, you will be the person running it, not just some part-time staff!

 There are some skills to learn but, most of all, find out if you enjoy the working environment and whether you will enjoy serving customers.

From a customer's point of view, waiting for an order, the business may look like it's quite easy. On the other side of the counter it's quite different. When it is busy and customers are queuing up to be served there is an adrenaline rush to prepare their orders quickly because you want to get them out of the door. Some people find that busy openings are very fast paced and they find it difficult to adapt.

There is also preparation work behind the scenes, including cleaning. A key question you have to ask yourself is do you enjoy cooking? Since the product is food and it's likely that *you* will have to prepare it, it helps if you like to get in the kitchen and cook for yourself and your family. You need to be able to imagine yourself working in a catering environment every day and be able to enjoy it.

Planning for the long term

Deciding to go into business should be a long-term plan since realistically only a long-term approach is likely to succeed. Building the business into a good reputable food outlet will take time. I do not advise anyone to go into any business for the short term. Dedication is needed and only the people who stay for the long term can reap the rewards.

A woman I know called Cindy owns a hairdresser's and has been in business for 20 years. She does not need to work anymore but continues to do so because she has grown fond of her customers. Ronnie owns the newsagent up the road from my establishment and has been in business for 19 years; he is also reaping the rewards. His beginnings in business were a struggle but he managed to get through the hard times and has come out on top.

Starting and running a business should be done with a long-term approach and vision. Although some people go into this type of business for a short time and do well, having a long-term plan will give you much more chance of reaching the goals of the business.

HAVING A CLEAR VISION

It's a good idea to have a clear picture of what you want. Food business owners who are starting out need to think of many good ideas and be creative in developing a good business. Do you aim to own a shop to satisfy fish and chip fans, and open additional outlets at the same time? Or do you want to begin with one premises and make it successful before you branch out? Having a clear vision in your mind supports the business as you have a definite direction.

Buying a food franchise

ADVANTAGES

If you want to open a food business but are unsure what type of food outlet to go into, and you also lack experience, then you may want to purchase a franchise. If you think you might not have a unique selling point in your business, or lack creativity, then a food franchise can be a solution. People are more likely to trust a franchise business as they often know about the company, and know that the food will be consistent. The reputation of the franchise company means that your business has instant credibility and an advantage over small independent businesses. Buying into a franchise means you will also get a lot of support from the company which is useful if you have little business experience. There will also be working systems in place and you will be taught how to run the operation.

DISADVANTAGES

Despite all these advantages, there are some negatives. Buying into a franchise is very expensive. Even if it is a reputable and successful business, it can still go wrong. Franchises do not go bust as often as independent food businesses, but there is still a risk. A franchise gives a proven working business format, but does not mean it is going to make your business a success.

There is an initial up-front fee and then a continual percentage is paid from the sales revenue. Some will charge an annual management fee and there are usually costs for any national advertising campaigns that are carried out. Some will charge for training. On top of all that, you will need to pay for all the usual expenses for the business like rent, utilities and staff wages.

There is very little control over the business because there is a strict agreement in place. You cannot implement any strategies or changes in the business, which means you cannot be creative. This limits your control which really means you will never be your own boss. You will usually be able to use only stock supplied by the franchisor. It is also very hard to sell the business, as whoever you're selling it to has to be approved by the franchiser. Above all, the business must be very successful to keep up with royalty fees and the usual overheads within a typical business.

Despite all the problems, it is a proven business model and the company is an established name. People already know and are aware of its products which gives it an edge over small food businesses.

Choosing a business format

When going into business you need to choose a format. Each format has differences in ownership, recording information and financial risks.

A SOLE TRADER

Being a sole trader is when you use your own name on a business in which you have the rights to all the profits and are personally liable for all the debts. This format is commonly used in small takeaway food businesses. It is easy to establish and the owner has full control; it is the simplest way to run a business as record-keeping and accounts are quite straight forward. The disadvantage is that you bear all the risks and the business is limited to the funds personally available.

A PARTNERSHIP

This format is when two or more people go into business together. Each partner needs to be registered as self-employed and shares the profits, debts, risks and costs of being in business. In some partnerships, members can contribute money to the business but not necessarily be physically involved in the operation. If one partner dies or goes bankrupt, the partnership ceases, but the business continues.

 A legitimate agreement should be produced properly by consulting a solicitor or accountant.

The problem with such a partnership is that the profits must be shared so the business needs to generate a substantial income. The people within the partnership should be people you can trust and genuinely like as business relationships can get complicated. There can be disagreements and a partner may want to leave the business, or one partner may contribute less effort to the operation.

A LIMITED COMPANY

This format allows the business to exist in its own right, so the finances of the company are separate from the personal finances of its owner. It can be set up through a solicitor or an accountant, but there is a lot more paperwork involved. The accounts must be audited and the business is liable for tax. The owners of the company receive a salary which is also liable for personal tax. A big advantage to this set up is that you limit your liability if the business goes under.

TRADING ON YOUR OWN

Most small food outlets are family businesses where people run an outlet with their spouse/partner. There are very few people who do it by themselves – I know only two people who have. Starting in trade for the first time on your own has many complications. It is a never-ending challenge because there is no one to lean on. Being in partnership or in a couple-run business means you can cover for and support each other.

 Being on your own will leave you to face all the risks and issues expected in a business. You will need a strong sense of independence, commitment and determination to make it work.

You cannot run the business entirely by yourself, without a helping hand. If you're serving customers on your own, it will be extremely difficult. You have to take orders and money from the customer, then the order must be cooked and prepared; two or three customers could be waiting for you to serve them whilst you're still working on the first order. Some customers who are impatient may even walk out. Customers are generally not sympathetic and notice when there is something wrong – like lack of staff. The business may also be affected with limited ideas and creativity to support its growth.

Things to consider when going into this type of business on your own:

☐ There is no one to cover your role when you're not feeling well or unable to work.

☐ You are unable to take even a short amount of time off.

☐ You will need more staff needed to keep the business running.

☐ There is no one to share work like cleaning (apart from paid staff).

☐ There is no one else to deal with any problems related to the business.

☐ You are responsible for all areas of the business.

As you can see, it is far from easy, but there are people who do it. There are also businesses that are set up and run entirely by staff without the owner being physically there. But going into the trade for the first time without support from a partner or spouse is very challenging.

Searching for a business

Nowadays the way to find anything is on the internet, and fast food businesses can be found through a business transfer broker which will have its own website. Some agencies sell all kinds of businesses from fish and chip outlets, coffee shops, restaurants, hotels and pubs to hairdresser's. Some specialise in one type of business.

When you make an enquiry, an agency will send out detailed information on the business you're interested in. It will usually include photographs, business turnover, type of tenure and sale price. There will also be a detailed description of the premises including the fixtures and fittings. There are many sites online that allow business owners to list their premises for sale.

Another useful way to find a business is in the newspaper, as many have a section on businesses for sale. Agencies advertise businesses for sale and as do people who want to avoid the expense of using a broker. Local newspapers will advertise businesses close to the area where you live.

One informal way to find a business is to have a friendly chat with the owner of a premises you're interested in. Ask them whether they are thinking of selling now or in the near future. I know people who have bought businesses this way. Some owners are glad that someone is interested and it saves them paying agency fees and advertising. You could use all these methods to look for a premises and when you find one that seems suited to your requirements, you can book to view the business.

When searching for a business you will need to take the following into account:

☐ **Location:** Is the premises in an area where you want to start a business? You will be spending most, if not all, your time running the business and the location must be ideal for you.

☐ **Type of tenure:** Are you interested in leasehold tenures or are you looking for a freehold business? If you want to have full ownership of the business and property, then you may want to avoid leasehold businesses. You will be able to spot which tenure the business is for sale at on its description.

☐ **Price:** It can be a good idea to have an idea in mind of what you would pay for a business. The amount will differ for freehold and leasehold businesses (see chapter 3) and whether you want to purchase a business with living accommodation.

☐ **Fixtures and fittings:** You should have a look at what comes with the business when it is purchased. There is normally a list of the main equipment along with other items. When people look at a premises they often overlook this, but the equipment plays a big part in the operation. See if the equipment is sufficient – it helps to compare the list from each business.

Summary

The beginning of the chapter will have made you aware of the challenges of running a business and that it is not an easy ride. You should also have some idea of whether you're fit to go into the trade. You will need to decide whether this career is suitable for you and whether you're willing to sacrifice certain things when running a retail business. The chapter has also gone into the different business set-ups and how to look for a trading business.

3
BUYING A SHOP

When purchasing a business, there is a lot of money to be invested. You have to be sure the business is the right one and worth taking a calculated risk on.

Buying freehold or leasehold

When you are buying a business, you will come across two tenures – leasehold and freehold. Both these tenures are very different and both have their advantages and disadvantages.

LEASEHOLD

Leasehold businesses generally include fixtures and fittings and an established trade. The lessee holds the property for a fixed number of years in accordance with the terms of a lease. This agreement is usually quite complicated and is issued by the lessor. The lessee pays rent (usually weekly) to the lessor and is obliged to comply with all the terms and conditions of the lease in order to stay in possession. The main terms and conditions are usually to keep up rent payments, insure the property and to keep it in good condition.

Leases usually exchange hands at prices which are much lower than freehold businesses, although the value can also be high for leasehold businesses that have a very high turnover. Leases offer little or no security for banks so it is generally very difficult to borrow to purchase a lease (you can use a freehold house to offer additional security to lenders).

Another disadvantage in leasehold tenures is that you will never own the building regardless of how hard you work. Even if you successfully ran the business for ten years and amassed a small fortune, you would still not own the building. Your dedication to the business will amount to nothing in terms of ownership. The point is, you will still be paying rent! For example, if a business was bought with seven years remaining on the lease and you wanted to continue running the business when the lease was coming to an end, you would have to pay an amount of money to the landlord to renew the lease. If you wanted to sell the business, but the turnover had reduced, you might not be able to sell for the price you paid for it.

FREEHOLD

Freehold businesses require a larger cash investment because of their value and cost. The capital required for the purchase will limit funds which could have been used for other expenses. The expense of freehold businesses includes a constant pressure to pay back lenders. Although freehold businesses are much more attractive to buyers because of their property value, the buyer can purchase it only if they have the necessary finances from banks and personal holdings.

THE LEASEHOLD ADVANTAGE

A leasehold agreement requires a much lower cash investment so there is less risk. It makes it much easier to start in the trade because of the lower costs compared with purchasing a freehold business. An advantage over freehold in terms of costs is that they're often easier to sell because they are more affordable. Some leasehold agreements may allow you to purchase the freehold at a later date, which means you can assess your performance in the trade without the risks of a freehold business.

THE FREEHOLD ADVANTAGE

The value of freehold means that lenders may be willing to lend over two thirds of the purchase price.

Freehold businesses provide good security to lenders as they know that if there is a repossession they will be able to get their money back.

The freehold tenure means that you will eventually have full ownership of the building. This is normally some years later, and can be worth more than you paid for it. Once the loan is paid off, there is nothing more to pay except bills.

I know a friend who ran his own shop for over a decade and decided he wanted to do something else with his life. The building was paid for, its value had increased and he received a good profit from his initial investment when he sold the premises. Another advantage if there is living accommodation with the business is that if it all goes wrong you still have a property. A lot of people know the value of freehold businesses as there are relatively few of them compared with leasehold tenures on the market. This means that a freehold business often generates more interest from potential buyers.

Researching locations

Just before I wrote this book, I had a customer who was a builder. We started talking, and I soon found out he used to run a fish and chip shop himself. He lasted only eight months. He told me he found it physically tiring and because business was unpredictable, he found it difficult to know when to order more or less stock. 'It was busy one week and quiet the next,' he said.

Apart from his ability to run an outlet, ensure the quality of service, and of course ensure his amount of commitment, a big reason for failure must have been the location. Describing the business as unpredictable gives tell-tale signs of the problem of location.

 When searching for a shop, people are immediately interested in the turnover, but the location is of equal importance and plays a crucial part.

All major retailers know the importance of a good location and will spend a lot of time and research scouting for suitable areas to open their next retail branch. Even if you plan to open in a holiday resort with a lot of potential business, the location must still be evaluated properly.

In any area the competition must be assessed, so look at locations you are interested in to see if there are other food businesses. Restaurants and catering outlets and even any supermarkets nearby need to be taken into account, as they are all part of the competition. A saturated location will mean less business to go around. Apart from good quality and service, the main reason for the success of most food businesses is the location. Too many businesses have failed due to poor locations. So you need to do your homework.

FINDING THE BEST TRADING TIMES

Your location will eventually determine your opening hours and the times you do the most business. If you open a premises that is very near busy pubs and nightclubs, there could be a lot of trade between the hours of 11 pm to 2 or 3 am. If it is near, or within, a residential area then there is likely to be a good amount of trade during lunch openings as well as teatime. If the premises is based in the centre of a parade of shops and near building and offices, they will usually generate foot traffic for you. There would be potential for busy lunches but will be less busy during the evenings. So the hours you plan to open for business must match the area and location of the premises.

CHECKING OTHER PLANNING

You may want to check with the local planning department to see if there will be any future development in the area. This will be useful especially in areas you are not familiar with. Developments could benefit or have a negative effect on your business. New building and office constructions may increase the level of pedestrian traffic but a new shopping complex nearby with its own food businesses will only increase the competition. An ideal location has plenty of pedestrian traffic either from a residential source or offices or is just in a spot that has a lot of passing trade, and is preferably somewhere that people can conveniently access your premises which means good available parking.

EVALUATING A PREMISES

When you have a found a premises you're interested in you can find out its exact address and take a look at the surrounding area. Good areas and locations are hard to find, so checking them first can save you the energy of having to look at the inside of a premises in an area with limited potential. If the travel time is long, it makes sense to book an appointment in which the premises and location can be evaluated together, to avoid a second trip.

When evaluating a premises in a particular location, run through these questions:

☐ Is there parking available outside the premises?

☐ If not, is there a car park nearby? If yes, does parking there require a charge or is it free? People will be more reluctant to park if it requires a fee to get to your premises. A premises without parking available will make it less convenient for people.

☐ Does the road have single yellow or double yellow lines? Double yellow lines will make it hard for customers to stop.

☐ Is there a neighbourhood of residents living close to the premises?

Catering outlets near where people live will be more likely to encourage trade especially when it does not require too much walking. Convenience is important to people. Do not always think that people prefer your products to another. Unless your premises or service is much better, people will choose the convenient alternative.

AREA AND POPULATIONS

The surrounding population is an important part of the location analysis. Get a map of the town or city and find where the premises is located. You should be able to see how big the area is and be able to estimate how big the population is which will tell you how much business you are able to get. You can find out exact population numbers by contacting the council in the area or on the internet.

A small town with significant amounts of competition may not pass the location assessment because of low population figures. A large population in the surrounding area of the premises, even with some competition, could be a good location for an outlet. Although rare, if you find a location with small amounts of competition, a thorough analysis would still be required. Population figures must be looked at, as well as parking availability and convenience.

Alarm Bell

Have a look at nearby shops and see if there are any up for sale – if there are lots it is a clear indication of a tried and tested area for new businesses. In other words, businesses have opened there and failed.

SPEND SOME TIME AT A LOCATION

Try to spend a couple of months researching a location and get a feel for the area, especially if you are a stranger to it. A city, for example, can be very different from a small town or village. If you drive only an hour or two away from where you live and spend some time in another town you will see many differences in area, landscape, style and age of houses. The people can also be different as each region in the country will have its own accent and dialect. You will also see that each individual town has its own history.

Proper location research is vital. Spend months doing it if you have to because you cannot afford to get it wrong.

ASKING VENDORS ABOUT THE BUSINESS AND LOCATION

You need to ask the vendor of a premises you're interested in some essential questions. For example, ask them how many sausages they go through in a week. If they go through more than five boxes, then they're doing quite well. (My mother's shop went through ten boxes of sausages a week!) Ask them the same about potatoes and fish. If they use more than 20 bags of potatoes and around five stone (31 kg) of fish, then they are very busy.

27

You may want to ask further questions about stock including burgers and other products. To guarantee accurate information, ask the seller to show you their recent receipts or invoices on the stock you're enquiring about. If they can prove their claims, then fine. But if they make an excuse, they may not be telling you the truth. Below are some more must-ask questions:

☐ **How long have you been running the business?**

If the owners have been operating the business for 15 years or more, you will know it should be quite established. They are likely to be more trustworthy and honestly answer your questions about the business and the property. This type of owners will also know the location and people in the area well. Ask them where most of the custom comes from. Is it passing trade, people living in the area, or a balance of both?

Alarm Bell

 Remember that there is no certainty. Even if an owner has been running a shop for a long time it still does not mean the business has been a success.

Owners that have been doing it a short time are more likely to have had problems. If someone has been running their shop for only two years, then there could be a negative reason for them to sell. You don't want to buy into a business that is on the verge of bankruptcy. You may feel you can turn a particular business around but you will still need to judge the prospects for that business.

☐ **What is your weekly turnover – can you show me your business accounts?**

Owners should have accounts showing the weekly turnover and outgoings for the time they have been in the business. They may also have profit and loss statements produced by their accountant.

☐ **Does the shop have a water meter?**

My own shop does not have one, which is great as I can use as much water as I want while paying a fixed price. Premises with a water meter will have to pay for the amount of water used. Finding a premises without a water meter is definitely a benefit, as water is used daily for cleaning. Also, water will be used daily if there is accommodation above the premises. Not having a water meter can help keep costs down.

□ What are the exact opening times of the business?

Be sure to get this information from the owners, as their opening times could have changed from the information the agency has given you. The vendor may have extended or reduced the opening hours. Know what days the business is closed. It is unusual for a premises to close on two or more evenings in the week. This indicates a failing business.

Be suspicious of businesses that have unusual opening times.

□ Do you have any trouble with youths?

Trouble from teenagers has long been a problem and is becoming worse; just read the local paper or watch the news. The antisocial behaviour of some teenagers affects people from those of their own age up to adults. Their negative energy is apparent in local communities and it is a serious problem that needs to be tackled. Youths who hang around on the streets can affect small shop owners; I witnessed them causing trouble when I worked for my mother. I remember a gang that used to drink alcohol every weekend, and sometimes we would get some trouble. It affects the business too, as some customers don't like to walk past groups of drunken teenagers.

Fish and chip shops and takeaways tend to open in the evenings, when they get most of their trade, and that is also the time when young people are on the streets. How bad the situation is will depend on the location. Teenagers often hang around together in a gang and pick spots where they can drink alcohol and take drugs. Quiet community areas seem to be the best places for them. A busy main road with noisy traffic isn't suitable as there is no place for them to sit. Be careful not to buy a business in a rough area which could turn into a nightmare with constant aggro from youths. (I have written a section offering some help with this problem in Chapter 10.)

□ Are any staff able to stay on when you have sold the business?

It is generally a good idea to keep some or all of the staff from the previous owners. They will know the operation well and be familiar with regular customers, and this will save you training new staff. The staff may even be able to teach you. Time is also saved in having to build rapport with customers.

☐ **Will you be able to stay and help the business for a short time?**

The vendors know the business well and it would be beneficial if they are willing to stay two to three weeks to help you out when you have bought the business. It would also be helpful for them to introduce you to the regular customers. The ice will then be broken which makes it easier to build a rapport.

CHECKING OUT THE TAKEAWAY PRICES

There is another classic mistake that shop seekers fall for – failing to find out the actual prices of food charged in the area they're assessing. For example, a price of a portion of fish and chips is quite different from one part of the country to another. The further south you go, the more expensive it is. Prices in the south can be double those in the North. Just look at property prices! You need to find out this information and it should be a part of your location evaluation.

You may think that when you take the business over you can simply raise the prices, but the locals would not be pleased. At the moment, fish and chips in Cheshire is around £3.30. In Lancashire it is currently around £2.80–£3. If you go to Bedfordshire, it is as much as £4.10. Around central London or surrounding areas, a portion of fish and chips can cost £5 or more! (For up-to-date fish and chip prices go to www.whatprice.co.uk/fish_chips.html)

The prices are very important as they dictate how much profit you can make from every sale. With higher pricing you can make more profit. Of course in any business you need to sell a lot to make a decent profit. Ten portions of fish and chips at £3 will amount to £30, but at £5 will be £50 – £20 difference.

Remember to look at prices of all food items in an area. Prices of food and everything else will eventually go up as this is the result of inflation, but if prices are low already it will take a long time. In the late 1980s, a portion of chips cost around 45p. Now I am selling them for £1. It has taken a long time to increase! So when viewing shops do look at the costs of fish and chips.

 There are some areas where fish and chips are charged at high prices. Try to go to these areas and stay away from places where it's not possible to charge a price that can generate a decent profit.

SPYING ON THE BUSINESS

Try not to take everything at face value. If the vendor of a particular shop tells you what their annual turnover is, it may seem impressive, but you will have to do some research. So do not be afraid to stand outside the premises to actually see how much business there is. Do it discreetly of course! Spend months researching if you have to – and I recommend doing it on different days and at different times each week. It's also a good idea to spend some time in the surrounding area to get to know it. Be prepared to walk away from the potential purchase if the results of your research prove negative.

 When observing the business, take a look at the passing trade that enters the premises and try to determine if those customers are locals or people passing through.

People may have just stopped for something to eat while driving through the town. Although passing trade is important, the regular trade from the nearby area is what you need. Passing trade is uncertain, unlike regular custom from people who live close by who could be long-term loyal customers.

If you find that the business going in is lower than you expected, but you see potential in the business, then you need to rely on your own judgement whether to buy that shop or move on. The best way is to be very sure of the potential of the business and this can be done only by spending enough time doing the necessary research.

Inspecting a premises

If you are going to invest your money in buying a business, then you need to make sure you inspect the premises properly. This includes checking the condition of the property and all the main and general working equipment. Once you have bought the business, there is nothing you can do if anything is wrong as it is generally the responsibility of the purchaser to make sure everything has been checked before paying for it.

CHECKING THE EQUIPMENT

Some old frying ranges can be close to the end of their working life and can take some time to be turned on. Often there is no remedy because of the age of the equipment. Ranges that have this problem tend to be even more difficult to turn on after they have had one or more days of rest. Older ranges may need to be replaced which costs a lot of money.

Alarm Bell

You must ensure the range (fryer) is working properly as a faulty one will postpone your opening date and will cost you money to fix.

Make sure main equipment, such as the potato peeler, works too, as these things are also expensive to replace. Some shops may have more than one to act as a spare, which should also be tested to ensure it operates.

In a fish and chip shop, the potato chipper is another main piece of equipment. You can take it apart by simply unscrewing the top and then having a look at the blades which cut the potatoes into chips. (Of course ask the vendor for permission first!) The condition of the blades will determine when they need to be changed. Blunt blades will not cut potatoes well and won't last long.

Be sure to test all equipment in the business so that you know that it is in good working order. You do not want to find once you have bought the business that some equipment does not work well, or does not work at all. General equipment like microwaves, refrigerators and freezers should also be checked. Working utensils, pots and pans should also be looked at because you will be using them daily.

It is a good idea to inspect not only the equipment, but also aspects of the property itself such as the condition of walls, floors, ceilings, to assess if any redecoration is required. If there is accommodation with the business you should have a good look at its condition.

TOP TIP When inspecting premises, see where the fryer is positioned. It is not good if it is against a wall and your back is towards the customer when you're cooking.

Facing the wall when cooking can make you appear rude and it is almost impossible to speak to customers while you're preparing their food facing the opposite way. Try to avoid this range position.

EQUIPMENT LIST

Below is the main list of basic equipment used in a typical fish and chip shop or burger bar.

Frying range – To fry chips and other food items

Potato peeler – Peels potatoes

Potato chipper – To cut potatoes into chips

Bain Marie – To keep sauces hot

Kebab grill – To cook kebab meats

Pizza oven – To make pizzas

Gas cooker – For sauces and general cooking

Microwave ovens – To heat up food

Fridges/Freezers – To store food and keep it fresh

CHECKING OUT ACCOMMODATION

When there is accommodation that comes with the business, it is wise to give the living area a thorough inspection. Even if you are not planning on living in it now, you may decide to at a later date.

Things to think about:

☐ Look at all bedrooms for size and the condition of ceilings, walls and carpets.

☐ Check the condition of the bathroom.

☐ If the accommodation has a kitchen, test the hob and oven and its general condition.

☐ Assess whether you think it is habitable. If you are not going to live in the property, then it is possible that the accommodation could be rented out, which will create another income. Try to assess whether it will be easy to let.

Getting the money to go into business

If you happen to be a very wealthy person and can afford to pay for a business with cash you're in luck – no money borrowed from the bank means no interest payments. You can earn profit from your business right away. Since you're not short of money, you can buy a few businesses and start a chain. But if you're like the majority of us then money must be borrowed.

BANKS AND LENDERS

If you're borrowing a large amount of money from a bank to buy a business, they will need to see an investment from you. The bank will usually lend around 50 per cent, but sometimes more than this. Interest rates are generally high for business loans like a commercial mortgage, in which a good deal would be around 2 per cent above base rate.

If you are buying a business from a business transfer agency they may be able to refer you to a lender as some agencies work with a particular bank. The rates are normally competitive. There are also loans available for up to £25,000 that generally need to be paid back in three to seven years.

Alarm Bell

Be careful not to over borrow or put yourself in a position of high risk that may put you in financial danger.

Try to do some research in finding the right bank or lender. Service standards can differ and as you will probably be with the lender for some time it makes sense to go with the right bank. Market trends will play a strong part in the ability for banks to lend. If there has been a decline in the general economy you may want to wait until it recovers before approaching lenders.

FAMILY AND FRIENDS

You should have a substantial amount of savings in your bank account and if you're going into business with your partner, hopefully they will also be able to contribute. Capital could be borrowed from family or you might be lucky and have friends who are close enough to lend you a large amount. Money borrowed from family can be interest-free. Do remember though that it can damage relationships when you're not able to pay them back in the time you said you would.

SELLING YOUR HOME

You may decide to sell your house to free up cash to buy a business, planning to live in the accommodation above the business and aiming to buy a home in the near future. I have never known anyone do it this way and would not recommend it to anybody – it is just too risky.

OTHERS WAYS TO RAISE FINANCE

Overdrafts

These come from your bank account and allow you to borrow up to a certain limit when there is no money in your account. They can be useful to cover short-term cash flow problems. Overdrafts offer more flexible borrowing than taking out a loan because you can repay them when it suits you, although they're not suitable for borrowing large amounts as their interest rate is normally higher than a personal loan.

Credit card

This can be a quick way to raise cash, especially if you take advantage of the introductory nought per cent interest on some cards. Many banks will issue credit card cheques. These give you instant cash, unlike the paperwork and application needed in conventional lending.

 Alarm Bell

 Be careful of hidden charges on seemingly great credit card deals.

Making a business plan

You will usually need a business plan to convince lenders that they are wise to invest their money in you. The plan should list your ideas and financial projections well. It must gather your ideas and objectives. It should have information on the market, what your competition is and if there is sufficient demand for your product. It should also contain realistic information on how the business will grow.

Alarm Bell

 Remember, the bank will usually lend only when it has a very good chance of getting its money back.

The business plan can also assist and measure the performance of the business; it can be reviewed and updated as the business develops.

There are businesses that have failed because of an inadequate business plan, which makes it more important to produce one that will be likely to help in business growth and is something that can be put into action to get realistic results. Accountants and advisers can provide advice in producing business plans, but is important to write it yourself. Information on business planning is also available at banks.

You may need at some point to present the plan to lenders – practise beforehand so that you come across professionally. This means knowing all the objectives in your business plan and includes understanding and explaining the financial forecasts. That way you will appear more confident and clear about the business which will help reassure lenders you are a good bet. The accounts from the vendor should be used, preferably from the past five years if available. This will demonstrate that the business already has profitable turnover and will display the trends.

A business plan will help because it:

☐ lists your objectives for the business

☐ shows you have a clear direction for the business

☐ shows your commitment to the business

☐ can be used to measure your progress

☐ gives the business more chance of success

A full business plan should include:

☐ executive summary

☐ short description of the business

☐ information about the product/service

☐ marketing and sales

☐ management and staff

☐ financial forecasts.

EXECUTIVE SUMMARY

Every business plan has an executive summary at the front of the document which gives an overview of the business plan. It is also the last thing to be written. It is like an introduction to your business, and its purpose is to summarise the key points of the plan which will prepare people for the plan's content. Acting like an organiser for the reader, an executive summary should be clear and to the point – no longer than two pages.

An executive summary also has to tempt the person reading it to be interested in the content of the business plan. If it fails to raise interest it may be left unread. Sometimes banks faced with a lot of lending requests will discard a plan with a weak executive summary fairly quickly. The information must be realistic as exaggerations, particularly in financial projections, may lead people not to believe you. Overall each section of the plan should be informative but to the point.

SHORT DESCRIPTION OF THE BUSINESS

This describes what your business sells, and its concept. You should describe the history of the business and its location. Point out the positive aspects and any problems and comment on how you are going to solve them. You should describe why you are selling your product and comment on who your customers are. Describe the current state of the industry and how you see its future. Try to give the reader an idea of where the business is heading and what will be accomplished over the next five years or longer. Remember this is a short description – don't include too much detail.

INFORMATION ABOUT THE PRODUCT OR SERVICE

This is your chance to explain your products and service clearly. Describe key features and benefits. Your reader will want to know what your product is and its advantages. Describe what will make your service different from other similar businesses. Explain the steps in your service process and the benefits you offer your customers. Include information about the main food products served. Explain how you will develop your product or service. The reader is interested in the highlights of your service and why it would be beneficial to people in the area.

MARKETING AND SALES

This is to explain the size of the market for the product. Most importantly, how you are going to advertise and promote your business. Describe any marketing strategies and methods you are using to increase your sales. You may want to show the pricing of products and some ideas on promotion. Lenders want to know your plans on advertising as it will have an effect on the performance of the business. Clearly define your target market. Describe your customers – you may want to include information such as age, gender, income and so on. Try to build a profile of the typical person you are targeting through your marketing campaign. The better you know your customer, the easier it is to reach them.

MANAGEMENT AND STAFF

In this section you should comment on who is going to manage the business and which people will work with you. You may want to include the CV or profile of everyone who will take part in managing your premises. Some banks base their entire investment decision on the management behind a venture. They expect a solid team that can run every aspect of the business. Your management section should clearly demonstrate who each person is, why he or she is on your team, and what they will do. This information is to convince the lender that your management team has enough skills or experience. You may want to talk about staff training and how that will support the operation.

FINANCIAL FORECASTS

Your financial plan will be examined carefully by the reader. The ideas and strategies discussed throughout the plan are important but the financial projections will show when you will be in profit. Forecasting what the business will make in the next three to five years will convince the lender the business has enough working capital to keep running. Forecasting aims to give the overall picture of income and expenditure that is expected over the year. It can be shown in a projected profit and loss account. You should also include a sales forecast which will predict how much money you will get from sales. Be realistic in your targets; avoid being too optimistic.

Submitting an offer and negotiation

You may want to get your finance set up before putting in offers or you can choose to look for financing after an offer is accepted. If a vendor is selling their business through a business transfer broker, the broker will negotiate for them. It is always a good idea to ask for the vendor's contact number so that you can negotiate directly and query information related to the business. If you're using a business broker, they can deal entirely with the negotiation on your behalf.

Trying to negotiate the purchase price is important as you will be dealing with large amounts of money. In general, the buyer wants to get the purchasing price as low as possible and the seller wants to sell their business at the best achievable price. Bear in mind that the vendor also has to pay the agency a commission fee for their service for finding a buyer. Agency fees are expensive – they charge around 3 per cent plus VAT on the purchase price.

My advice in submitting an offer would be to go in low and also have a set figure in mind of the most you would pay. If the negotiation goes over your set figure it will be easier to walk away than if you don't have one. Negotiation can be tricky as people can be inflexible: often they believe that once the sale price is set it should be sold close to, or at, the asking price. Negotiation is not a breeze. If problems arise in the process and you are not happy with an aspect of it, remember you have a choice to stop and walk away. Do not allow yourself to be pressurised as businesses come on the market all the time and it takes patience to find the right one.

 Try to appear confident and in control of negotiation.

When buying a shop through an agency, you will still be allowed access to the phone number of the vendor as it is expected that you will form a relationship. The agency can act between you and the vendor, but you can still deal with the owners directly to discuss any issues. Bear in mind that the agency is mostly on the side of the vendor and will want to help them sell at the best price. When negotiating or dealing with the vendor or agency, remember the following.

REMAIN CALM, IN CONTROL AND NON-PERSONAL

The seller will pick up on your confidence. You will appear more in control when the vendor knows you are not going to allow yourself to be personally attached to making the deal. This does not give an impression that you are not a serious buyer, it just means you will be more in control and an effective negotiator. You could prepare yourself before engaging in negotiation.

BE SURE TO KNOW EXACTLY WHAT YOU WANT OUT OF THE TRANSACTION

This might be purchase price, stock or furniture. With the purchase price, know exactly how much you are willing to pay for the business. It is important you can stick to your decision. There should be no transaction if the price has gone over the set amount. Write down what you need from the deal on a piece of paper and keep it close by as a reminder when speaking on the phone or in person to the vendor.

IT'S IMPORTANT TO ASK FOR WHAT YOU WANT

For example, you may want the seller to knock off a fair amount of money from the asking price or perhaps to throw in some business stock with the sale. If the vendor refuses on the price reduction, perhaps they would take off half the amount you suggested. The same goes for stock. For a swift sale and satisfaction for both parties, the vendor should be flexible.

The result should be acceptable to you both, as the best negotiation is when both parties win. Vendors who show very little flexibility hinder their chances of a sale. You must spend time thinking about whether you are going into a good deal and be sure to avoid going along with an unfair transaction just because you fell in love with a particular business.

 Do not let emotions get in the way when negotiating. Logic should always come first.

REMEMBER YOU'VE GOT AN ADVANTAGE

Keep in mind that people wanting to sell their business may have been in the trade for a long time and now want out. They may also have other reasons to sell. These reasons, be they good or bad, should really work to your advantage. You are the one with the cash, you are not attached to any business constraints, and can easily wait for a better shop to come along. Your position should put you in more control.

NEGOTIATING ON STOCK

There might be some stock left in the business which the vendor can not use. The stock could be negotiated in the deal (include it in the purchase price) so that once the business is taken over, you're ready to start trading. If the vendor is unwilling to put stock in the sale, you could negotiate buying it at a discounted price. When the deal is complete the owners should be there to hand over the keys to the premises and that is the chance to check the amount of stock agreed.

NEGOTIATING ON FURNITURE

If there is living accommodation above the premises there could be furniture, beds, wardrobes, a dining table and chairs. If the vendor lives there you could try to negotiate those items in the deal which will save you moving your own into the property or having to buy new. When I bought my business the accommodation was large with three good-sized bedrooms. The vendor left me two very good quality beds, wardrobes and other useful furniture. It saved me buying my own. Some sellers may even be pleased that you want their furniture, saving them the cost of having to hire a removal van. Be sure to check that the furniture agreed is all there when the keys to the premises are collected.

FLAWS IN THE PROPERTY

If somewhere inside the property needs repair, it can be pointed out to the vendor so that a price reduction can be negotiated.

Alarm Bell

If there is accommodation above the premises don't forget to check the ceiling area on the ground floor for any water damage.

FLAWS IN THE BUSINESS

You can negotiate on limited parking availability, business competition and low turnover. If you do find something about the business that can reduce the purchase price, the vendor should be informed and discuss it with you, so don't be afraid to ask. Although vendors should compromise some can be inflexible. If you believe there are quite a few imperfections to the business and the negotiation is not positive, then it may be wise to move on.

The survey

The bank will require a survey (at your expense) to see that the property is sound, and will value it against the purchase price. The survey will contain a description of the property, whether there is accommodation and its tenure. It will also describe the condition of the premises and comment on the competition in the close area where the business is located. It will usually include photographs inside and outside the premises. There will be plenty of useful information about the business. It may even point out things that you have overlooked.

The survey is your tool to assess the business and property for its condition, its competition and price. If the survey identifies any problems you could use them to your advantage in price reduction. The survey is carried out by trained surveyors and they will point out any problems in construction, any dampness or movement in the property. They also value the business correctly at current market value.

When there are significant issues, you must decide whether the business is the one to purchase or not. The survey fee will not be wasted if you do not decide to go ahead. There will be a lot more sacrifice and regret if you buy a business with problems which were pointed out to you in a survey report.

THINKING CAREFULLY BEFORE YOU BUY

Buying and running a business isn't for everyone because of its time-consuming nature, its challenges and the energy and commitment needed to make it work. Thinking clearly before buying something with a large amount of money is not being too careful, but smart. And that goes for buying an investment property, a new residence, an expensive car or anything else. Even if an offer you have submitted has been accepted and you have instructed your solicitor and set up a loan with the bank, you can still decide to withdraw your decision. Unless you have put pen to paper, you still have a choice.

Be sure to have researched the location of the premises thoroughly and inspected the property carefully. If you are unsure, go and visit it a couple more times. Being in business is like being in a marriage – you have to be committed. It is not unheard of for people to divorce after nine months of marriage, although in business it is not so easy to separate. Getting out of business early can lead to unpaid debts, loss of initial investment and in the worst case scenario to bankruptcy, which will seriously affect your credit rating. In business you must be able to deal with never-ending challenges and lots of work, just like a married couple has to work hard to sustain a happy relationship.

Instructing a solicitor

Once an offer has been accepted, you need the services of a solicitor to conveyance your purchase. If you are buying through an agency, they should be able to refer you to one. I would advise you to find your own solicitor and phone around for quotes. You may notice there is quite a difference in the cost of the services of one solicitor compared with another.

Some solicitors will charge more for transfer of ownership of businesses than for ownership transfer of a home because they view it as requiring more work. Also terms on a leasehold tenure can be complex. Others will charge more reasonably. Use the *Yellow Pages* and call some of the local solicitors in your area. When you are happy with a quote you have been given you will need to pass on your details to your chosen solicitor.

A solicitor will be looking out for your interests – apart from transferring ownership they are there to protect you.

When you meet your solicitor to sign papers he or she may offer some last-minute advice on the business. There could be positive or negative comments about the business. As I said, the solicitor is there to protect you and it is their job to offer advice that may be helpful. If all seems OK to you, the deed is signed to transfer ownership of the business so that contracts can be exchanged.

Getting the right insurance

You will need to buy insurance cover to protect the premises and its equipment. Shops without shutters, for example, have a higher risk for potential damage than premises that are protected when they are not open. A flat roof has a much more expensive premium as it is generally less efficient than a sloping roof in terms of drainage.

You can obtain quotes yourself or use a broker. It may be easier to use a broker as they will be able to get a competitive rate and save you time in ringing a list of insurance providers.

Insurance is a necessary expense to provide coverage for the following:

- damage to the premises

- contents, such as stock, equipment and personal contents

- loss of revenue, cash

- personal accident

- employer's liability (this cover is needed even when using part-time staff)

- frozen foods

- public and products liability.

Cover such as loss of cash, property damage and personal accident should be in your insurance policy. Employer's liability is compulsory if you are employing anyone – even part-time or casual workers. Being a business owner carries a legal responsibility to the employees, customers and the public.

You could be sued if a worker or member of the public is injured as a result of your negligence. For example, if a customer or employee slips on a wet floor in the premises and hurts themselves badly, it would be the fault of the owner. Your insurance cover would pay out any compensation or legal costs if required. Also if someone is injured and awarded personal injury compensation, the NHS can claim to recover the costs of hospital treatment.

Finding out about the premises

Try to find out as much information as you can about the business from the vendors and from inspection. However, it is not possible to know all about the premises as you have not run the business yet. Only after spending some time in the property will you be familiar with the equipment in the business and the building. So your key source is the vendors. Don't be afraid to ask them every question you can think of. It shows you care about what you're paying for and take going into business seriously. They should answer all your queries if they want to have a successful sale.

LEARNING HOW TO USE THE EQUIPMENT

Make sure you know how to use the equipment in the premises. Some cash registers can be complicated. Learn how to operate the fryer and know exactly how to turn it on and off safely, as you don't want to leave it on overnight. You will have to check that the gas is turned off after every opening.

 Remember safety! Every catering outlet should have two fire extinguishers: find out where they are and how to use them.

The premises should also have a fire blanket. Depending on the individual outlet, there may be other equipment like pizza ovens, coffee machines, kebab equipment and so on. Be sure to ask the vendor to show you how they operate – it will also prove that the equipment works. When I bought my premises, I made sure the vendor taught me how each piece of equipment worked.

RECORDING INFORMATION FROM THE VENDOR

Ask the vendor to write everything about the operation of equipment and the shop clearly in a small notebook. Then if you are unsure about anything, just refer to the book. Ask them to list details of all suppliers and the contact details of the gas engineer who services the range, chipper and potato peeler. Ask them to list any other useful contact numbers related to the business.

It is also a good idea to ask the vendor for their own contact details so that if a query can't be answered you can reach them for assistance. Get a home telephone number and mobile number. They may have an email address or another preferred method of getting in touch.

Unexpected problems regarding the property or business may occur and the vendors can usually help.

A book with relevant information and contact details is very useful. You will find that you refer to the book quite frequently. The range could suddenly become faulty, for example, or you may need to talk to a supplier. It is wise to make a copy of the book as a back-up in case you lose it. Or perhaps even input it on a computer.

Fitting out your shop

An empty shop or even a house can be turned into a food outlet. Shops that open this way can be very successful, although you must be careful and be one hundred percent certain of the potential of the location.

You really do not want to spend thousands fitting your own shop from scratch and find you don't get any return. If you get it right, it could be a very successful shop and the whole transformation process will have been worthwhile.

APPLYING FOR PLANNING PERMISSION

You must contact the council for planning permission – only once approved can the fitting process begin. The council will look at the amount of fast-food businesses in the area you're applying for and decide whether there is room for another one. If the area is already saturated with food businesses, permission may be denied. This is because a new food business will affect similar businesses in operation causing negative outcome on trade and revenue, which puts those other businesses at risk and causes problems for the area.

Another thing they may look at is the location of the premises or the property itself. They will decide whether the premises is suitable to be transformed into a food business. They will want to know if there is anybody living next door or close to the premises, and assess if the activity of a food business will disturb or affect other people. The council will need to approve colour schemes in the renovation of the premises and sometimes even for the signage of the shop front.

Shop design

There are companies that specialise in frying ranges and catering equipment and can design and turn an empty shop into a fast-food outlet. They can come up with a plan for your premises with your requirements and offer designs to create a practical working space. Their service also includes kitchen designs and the fitting of professional catering sinks.

Decide what you want the premises to look like. Work closely with the shop fitters and be sure to get the desired result.

If you are transforming a location from empty shop to food establishment you may want to create a very modern look, or put your own signature design on it so that it can bring something new to the market. With modern designs only the best working equipment – including top-of-the-range fryers – will be suitable. Modern shop designs and layouts are impressive and are necessary to create some buzz in the area. By creating the best you will be likely to attract people to use a new food service.

Using a shop fitting service which specialises in fitting small fast-food businesses can speed up the process as they will have contacts for engineers, electricians and other tradespeople. There will be more chance of a definite date to complete the project. They may even do a better job than if you go down the route of finding individual workmen to carry out the shop fitting and its renovation.

FITTING A FRYING RANGE

You can hire a qualified Corgi gas engineer who has had experience in fitting frying equipment to do the job. They will measure up in the premises and tell you where a range can be fitted. They will give you a quote – it will not be cheap. A range is very expensive, but will last 20 years or longer.

Installing your own burner means you can install modern equipment, as many ready-to-trade shops usually have older models. Most modern burners are controlled by an electronic unit which provides automatic ignition, flame-failure protection and an indicator lamp to confirm that the pilot light is lit. The temperature of the pan is controlled and operated by a thermostat which will display the temperature levels.

Modern fryers should have an automatic function installed to disable the heat in case of temperature levels exceeding 425 degrees Fahrenheit. Chip boxes and display cabinets are electronically heated to keep ready-food hot. (Some older ranges are not able to keep heat in the chip box.)

Some modern burners have a safety panel built in to monitor the performance of the extraction of gas fumes. If the extraction level is not safe, the safety panel reacts by automatically shutting down. The pans on a modern range are generally more efficient, which has the advantage of reducing the gas bill and reducing NOx gases. (These gases can contribute to greenhouse emissions, smog and acid rain.) The main advantage is that they are much more economical and some have built-in filtration to keep the oil in good condition. If a range does not have this function, separate equipment can be used.

FINDING EQUIPMENT

There are many catering equipment suppliers – you can find them online (search for 'catering equipment') and in the *Yellow Pages*. Most websites are well set up with pictures and pricing available. They are convenient to buy from and some even deliver free of charge.

FINDING TRADESPEOPLE

When trying to source your own builders and tradesmen, you may want to find ones who have experience of fitting out a shop – they will be more efficient to work with and can produce work that will better match your criteria. Work closely with them and make sure they know your exact requirements for the design of the shop. Be clear about what kind of establishment you're aiming to create. Will it have eat-in facilities or offer extra outside seating? Will the shop serve a range of food from fish and chips and pizzas to kebabs? If so, it should show in the decoration, menu design and feel of the premises.

CHOOSING THE DÉCOR

The décor should be bright and welcoming. The walls and even the floor should be tiled. Of course other materials can be used, but the key is to make it look tidy, and easy to clean and maintain. In a food place, the colour scheme should be light and represent the feeling of food. Colours such as light blue or even red work. Avoid dark colours.

The lighting should be bright and never dim. The design of the shop front and signage is important as it is what people see from a distance. It gives the message of what you're selling. Try to use an original name for the business. A well-designed shop front will create the image of the business and is the most direct advert to people who pass the premises. Its detail should be as important as the interior of the premises.

Complying with requirements

When a shop is transformed into a food-selling business it must comply fully with legal requirements; it must satisfy the standards set by the authorities. (These issues can of course be avoided when buying a ready-to-run business.)

LIGHTING AND VENTILATION

The premises should have adequate lighting, either natural (daylight) or electrical. It needs to be well lit in the evening by fluorescent lighting, which should be bright and welcoming.

 The premises needs to have enough ventilation – either natural, such as windows, or vents.

The preparation room should be of a good size to allow the movement of air and to provide a comfortable working space. Electrical extractor fans and an opening back door will also help ventilate the shop. Toilets need to have some ventilation too.

WASH BASINS AND STORAGE FACILITIES

There should be an adequate number of washbasins, used only for cleaning hands. There should be a separate sink for washing food, based in the kitchen area. Every sink for food washing must have an adequate supply of hot and cold water. The water must be of drinking quality. These facilities must be clean and maintained. Drainage must be satisfactory and constructed to avoid the risk of contamination. There should be good storage areas for working utensils and equipment.

PREPARATION AREAS AND STAFF ROOMS

Areas for food preparation should be designed to allow good food hygiene practices which reduce contamination risks. These areas need to look pleasant and be reasonably comfortable and safe to work in. The construction and size of your premises should allow easy cleaning and disinfection. There should be good spaces and facilities to store food at the correct temperatures.

Staff should also have access to a room to enable them to change into their working clothes. This room should also be somewhere secure to put their belongings.

Construction requirements

CEILINGS

These areas and any overhead fixtures should prevent dirt from building up and reduce condensation. The area must be finished so that it reduces the growth of mould.

FLOOR

Materials used for the floor must be easy to clean and must not allow water to pass through. Flooring materials should be non-slip for health and safety purposes to protect your staff and customers. Where appropriate floor surfaces must allow adequate surface drainage.

WALLS

These surfaces must be easily maintained, preferably tiled, and be easy to clean. Walls should consist of materials that do not allow fluids to pass through them.

SURFACES

Any area where food is handled, including equipment, should be easy to clean and disinfect. Surfaces need to be made of materials that are smooth, non-toxic and corrosion-resistant.

Overseeing the work

Be realistic in your budget for the project and have your builders give you a quotation of how much it will cost to do the job. Get a date from them for when the project will be completed. The longer it takes to renovate, the more money it will cost you as you will still have to pay rent and council tax.

It takes patience to fully renovate an empty shop to an acceptable standard as it can take quite some time. It is best to take care of every detail in the shop and be sure it matches your required design and that the decoration is complete before you start to trade.

 Remember, the shop design needs to make a lasting impression on first-time customers. It is better to add all finishing touches to the premises so that it is ready before it opens to the public.

THE DISADVANTAGES OF FITTING OUT YOUR OWN PREMISES

The route of transforming a commercial premises into a food outlet is risky, because you do not know whether there will be any actual business. Other shops that are trading may have been established for years. Many will have built long relationships with a strong customer base. Less successful outlets will have at least a basic turnover.

There are uncertainties in business and you should research thoroughly to minimise risks. Unless you have plenty of available cash and can stomach a loss, I do not recommend this form of opening a premises. It will cost you thousands to renovate, and will drain your energy working on the project before you have even opened for business. If you decide to sell later, it may be difficult. Remember that a business is valued by its turnover and its market value could be disappointing because it is an under-established business.

Registering your premises

If you run a food establishment you must tell the local authority. People starting a new food business must inform the authorities at least 28 days before doing so. (Certain premises may be exempt if they are already registered for food law purposes.)

Surviving the first week of trading

The first day of opening through to the end of the working week will usually be difficult. You have never run the shop before, so you will have your first full contact with the premises, the working equipment and staff. The customers who come in will notice a new face, or should I say owner. You will give the business a new identity which will be different from that of the previous person.

If there are staff who were kept on after the business was sold, or new staff recruited, they will be working with you for the first time and getting a feel of what you are like to work for as a boss. And you will of course be observing them and getting an idea of what they are like as employees. It will usually be a tough week, but it will also be enjoyable if the openings make a profit and things go smoothly.

MAKING A GOOD IMPRESSION

You must try to get the first week right. Regular customers will turn up and have a taste of your service for the first time. Your chance to make a good impression on them is during this first week of trading.

When I bought my premises, the vendor agreed to help me in my first three weeks of trading. He introduced me to all the customers, but mostly to the regulars who came in. I was under a lot of pressure trying to get used to the working environment and getting to know all these people. The customers were friendly, but it was sometimes difficult to have a good conversation with people I was meeting for the very first time.

Alarm Bell

There is only one chance to impress your customers. Harsh as it sounds, if regulars are not impressed with your product, service or you, they may not come back. It is vital to make a good impression on people during your first week.

BUILDING RELATIONSHIPS

When your operation and delivery are well planned they should go well, but your food and service must be good too. After a hectic first week, the pressure in the second week will ease off a little and a little more as each week goes by. This is because you will have begun to get used to the operation, the staff and the customers.

The truth is that the first three months of trading are a constant challenge to impress and keep hold of existing customers. Get it wrong early on and you will hurt the turnover. In these stimulating months you will meet people, get to know customers and slowly build a relationship with them. When relationships are established, you have truly got your regular customer base.

You need to make a positive mark as the new owner of the business. During this time, your working relationship with staff will have developed. If you're in business with your spouse or partner, there will some change in your relationship as it will have been a challenging three months. You want to make sure that the business heads upwards and not in the opposite direction.

As you now know, the risks are high. It does not matter how well you plan the project – the completion of the shop does not guarantee expected turnover. However, there are people who have successfully managed to make their projects work and ended up with a business that proved to be a success.

Summary

We have looked at types of tenure and the advantages and disadvantages of them. Location is a crucial aspect to get right and also the pricing of your products. The full buying process has been described including the main points of negotiation and inspecting of a premises. When buying a business you need to know everything about it because once it belongs to you the vendors are not obliged to answer your queries. We have also covered how to fit out your own shop and requirements of such a renovation. The first week in business up to the next three months will be challenging, but essential to get right. There must be a strong intention to kick start the business from the beginning.

4
FINDING SUPPLIES FOR YOUR BUSINESS

Choosing fish

Most of the fish landed in the UK are from Scottish ports but the majority of fish consumption is in England and Wales. In total there are about 280 ports around the country. Fish and chip shops are the dominating outlet of the seafood market. The cost of fish is rising because of high demand and known health benefits of eating it.

Alarm Bell

Fish can come fresh or frozen. Frozen fish can be used for up to three months but fresh fish should ideally be used within two to three days.

The most popular seafood in retail is cod, which explains the expense of stocking it. People in Britain eat one third of all cod consumed in the world. The demand for cod has caused supplies to become scarce, and the expense of stocking it makes it hard to have much profit margin so many fish and chip shops use other types of fish. Alternatively, they increasingly offer other types of fish on their menu while still serving cod.

Fish is normally ordered as fillets. Fillets are convenient and speed up the preparation process in the industry. Skinned and boned fillets are ready for frying and need only some minor checks for bone.

There are outlets that order a whole fish, which makes its preparation much more time consuming. Although more time and work is needed, the advantage of using a whole fish is that there is more control of portion size.

COD

This white fish has flaky flesh and has long been a popular frying fish, and though over-fishing has put strain on its supply, it is still available throughout the year. The cost of buying cod has increased dramatically because of demand for it and its limited supply. It lives in the cold northern waters of the Atlantic and is available fresh or frozen.

It can be cooked in a number of ways as it is very versatile. Cod is a favourite fish for the Portuguese; they have hundreds of recipes for it and regard it as one of their country's treasures. The liver from cod is also used to make cod liver oil which is rich in vitamins A and D as well as omega-3.

HADDOCK

A member of the cod family, it is an extremely good substitute for cod as the fish are very similar in flavour. Haddock and cod are the most common types of fish to be served in fish and chip shops, along with plaice. Haddock grow rapidly and are plentiful in supply. This white fish is also delicious when smoked.

PLAICE

This is a flat fish used in fish and chip outlets. It cooks quicker than other white fish and is regularly eaten in Denmark where they like it pan-fried or as a hot or cold open sandwich. Its flesh is soft and has a delicate flavour. It can be bought whole or in fillets all year round.

POLLACK

Sometimes named 'pollock', this is a strongly-flavoured white fish and is a versatile alternative to haddock and cod.

HAKE

This is a deep-sea member of the cod family also suitable for deep frying, although it tends to lose flavour quite quickly so only the freshest fish should be used. Low demand for hake means that it is cheaper in comparison with more popular fish like haddock or cod.

MONKFISH

This fish from the northwest Atlantic tastes better than it looks. It is a delicate fish, has a great flavour and is suited to frying.

HUSS

This fish, which is dense and meaty, is also known as rock salmon. It is a popular frying fish in some regions of the country, but virtually unheard of in other areas. Huss comes from the dog fish family, so the name of rock salmon was created to make it more commercial.

LEMON SOLE

This popular flat fish originates from shallow waters around Northern Europe. It is commonly used in cooking and is often pan-fried.

SALMON

A popular fish in cooking. It can be eaten in many ways and is suited to frying.

CHOOSING WHAT FISH TO OFFER

There are other types of fish that can be used and your range will depend on your outlet. Will you offer a diverse range of fish or a few popular types? Haddock and cod are the most commonly-used fish in fish and chip shops. Sometimes customers need encouragement to try other types of fish. I would recommend that you stock different types of fish to add more choice and variety. Giving customers more choice will also make your establishment different from outlets that offer limited varieties of fish.

FISH BATTER

This is for fish-frying and can be bought as a mix or home-made. There are many types of batter available, including gluten-free and even an organic version. The quality of the batter affects the taste of the fish, so it is important to select the right one. Ideally you should test different batters to assess their quality. Fried fish as a main product must have all the right components to create the best possible product.

FISH PRICES

The cost of fish tends to fluctuate throughout the year owing to supply and demand. Popular fish like cod that is over-fished tends to increase in price every year. General frying fish such as haddock is plentiful in supply and the price through the course of the year is mainly affected by demand.

The price of fish is usually cheaper during the early months of the year when there is less demand. During moderate demand from the market, haddock can cost around £38 for a box of 45 fillets skinned and boned. In months of reasonable demand it can cost around £42. Fish is in high demand during the months of October-December when fish and chip outlets are at their busiest; then a box of haddock can cost around £48. (There are around 11,000 fish and chip shops in Britain that are ordering fish to fill this busy period.)

Fish that is low in demand, such as whiting, can be very cheap to get hold of. It also looks very similar to popular fish like haddock and cod. The problem is that it loses flavour quickly and customers can tell the difference. I have never stocked whiting as a substitute for haddock, although I have sometimes been supplied it without my consent because of limited stocks of haddock.

Frozen fish fillets can be bought at cheaper prices than fresh fish. I have used them only once, when suppliers had no fish available after December because fishermen were still on their holidays. But frozen fillets lack flavour compared with fresh fish which is the reason why their prices are so low. I recommend you buy fresh – it is quality produce that costs more, but keeps customers satisfied.

Choosing potatoes

The British are the third largest consumers of potatoes in Europe with only Portugal and Ireland eating more. Around 10 per cent of all potatoes eaten in the UK are sold through fish and chip shops. There are around 80 varieties of potato grown in this country.

Fresh potatoes make the best chips, although some takeaways like to use frozen chips for convenience. The flavour from chips that are frozen doesn't compare with freshly made 'chippy' chips, although a burger business might be able to get away with using ones that are frozen.

Potatoes that do not have too much moisture will make chips with a good flavour and texture. Try to avoid waxy potatoes with low dry matter which will fry too dark. Product knowledge will come in useful so talk to potato merchants (most people in the trade call them 'the potato man').

You may want to visit a merchant to see how things are done on the farm.

 Some potato merchants offer a range of supplies from potatoes to fruit and vegetables. Some even supply peas, gravies and soft drinks at competitive prices. Instead of using several suppliers you can use the potato merchant to supply you with stock at reasonable prices.

The following potatoes are suitable for chipping:

MARIS PIPER

This is the favourite chip shop potato. It has cream skin, cream flesh and its texture is floury. It rarely changes colour when cooked and is truly a versatile potato. It is suitable for boiling, baking, roasting and is a favourite for deep-fat frying. It creates the perfect chips, its flavour is unmatched and it is preferred by many fish and chip shop owners.

MARIS PEER

This potato has cream skin and cream flesh, eyes shallow to medium.

MARIS BARD

This is oval and medium size with white skin, white flesh and shallow eyes. This is a first early variety. It is good for early chipping.

VICTORIA

This early main crop variety has proved to be popular for fish friers. Its early maturity and reliability in storage give growers the opportunity to provide the customers with a supply all year round.

DESIREE

This potato has red skin and light yellow flesh. It has a firm texture and is excellent for chipping.

KING EDWARD

This potato has white skin with pink colouration and cream to pale yellow flesh. It also has a floury texture. These potatoes are excellent for making chips.

AGRIA

A large potato which has yellow flesh and is quite clean so it doesn't need much work.

MARKIES

This Dutch potato is becoming popular in the frying trade. It is a very good size potato, clean and very reliable. Some fryers think there is more taste to Maris Piper but Markies serves well as the next best alternative.

SANTE

These potatoes are yellow in skin and flesh. They are dry and firm.

PREMIERE

A first early variety which has a firm dry texture.

SAXON

This potato is firm and its texture moist. It is a second early variety which is suited for chipping, but is also extremely good for mashing.

FIANNA

Has smooth white skin.

CARA

A very robust variety which has some red colour on the exterior. It is suitable for a variety of culinary uses.

WILJA

This light yellow potato is suitable for chipping but is better for mash.

POTATO PRICES

The price of potatoes drops around the months of June to September. When winter approaches the prices rise and can become ridiculously high in December. I have known a bag of potatoes in December to cost around £8. In the summer the same 25kg of potatoes (usual size) can be bought at around £5.50.

Prices can vary from region to region and by variety of potato. The price will also differ according to the amount of work needed and general quality when fried. From experience, it is better to use potatoes that are good quality and don't require much work.

POTATO MERCHANTS

There are many potato merchants who can supply you and, with persistence, you should be able to source some quality potatoes at a reasonable price, but the usual influence of supply and demand will affect their cost. In quiet intervals in the trade, merchants can also lower their prices, so try to negotiate.

Be careful as some suppliers will give you potatoes that are not at the right standard and need a lot of preparation, which will produce more waste. Cleaning bad potatoes with a knife can be the longest part of any preparation done in a fish and chip shop. The more bags of potatoes needed for the day, the more work is needed to prepare them.

Some potato suppliers will give you very bad potatoes and not all suppliers are honest. When I receive a delivery of potatoes that is not up to standard, I contact my supplier immediately to take them back and to bring some acceptable stock. If a supplier lets you down frequently, it may be best to find another merchant.

OTHER CHIP PRODUCTS

There are alternatives to potatoes, such as vacuum-packed fresh chips. Makers of this type of product claim that the chips are as fresh as normal chips made from fresh potatoes, that there are no bits that can come in chips made the normal way, and that they will keep the oil cleaner and lasting longer.

They were clearly created for convenience as all the work is done without having to peel potatoes, tidy or chip them. The size of chip is also good. Using this sort of prepared chips is just the same as using frozen fries – they are convenient and easy to prepare. Some suppliers even stock potatoes that are already peeled.

Whichever method you use to produce chips it needs to be suited to your particular establishment. From my point of view, using fresh potatoes will always make the best chips to complement fish. Though for speedy preparation, you may want to stock chip products that are ready to be cooked without having to do so much preparation.

Choosing pies

Pies are an essential part of fish and chip shops and one brand that has been around since the early days of the trade is Holland's pies. The company began to grow around the same time as fish and chips were becoming common in the 1920s. It was established in 1851 and is the leading brand in Lancashire for pies, dominating 85 per cent of the chip shop market in the north west.

There are other pie-making companies such as Pukka pies and Shire pies (a list of pie brands can be found in the Appendix).

All pies should be tried and tested for quality. I always assess new food products before I sell them to my customers.

Whichever company you use, you need to evaluate the pies for taste, size and freshness. The pie market is a very competitive business in its own right – there is a large range of pies available, and the prices differ for each brand. Some less expensive brands seem to taste just as good as the well known, and using them will save on costs. Recently I tried pies from a different supplier; they are cheaper to stock and the standard is just as good as the ones I was using.

 Try pies from a number of different suppliers; assess the products on taste and the cost of stocking them.

Choosing sausages

Sausages are inexpensive to stock although the prices charged to customers have risen over the years. They are also quite versatile in the way they are served. They can be eaten on their own or in a bun. They can also be served with chips or covered in peas and gravy and even battered.

It is essential to buy the right ones as not all sausages taste the same. Some are spicy and there are differences too in firmness, texture and overall quality. I tend to go for pork-made sausages and not those made from beef, as pork is the meat most often used to make sausages. Beef sausages tend to brown easily and can appear over-cooked.

There are many brands of sausages on the market, and you can also get them from your local butcher. Blakemans, McWhinney's and Tasty-Bake are some of the well known-brands (see the appendix for suppliers).

Choosing burgers

The taste and quality of burgers should be of a good standard. Profit margins on burgers, like sausages, are very good. They are cheap to stock and generate high profits when you sell a lot. When the right supplier is found, a box of 48 burgers can be bought for as low as £6. If a single burger is sold for £1.50, you would need to sell only four burgers to have covered the cost of buying the full box.

There are different sizes of burgers available, and it is best to stock a range of them. Do bear in mind that beef burgers do not all taste the same. When I bought my premises I decided to change the burgers instead of using the same as the previous owner. It was a mistake – some regular customers noticed the difference and were not pleased about it. I quickly changed them back.

 Listen to your customers and let them be the judges on quality.

Beef burgers can also be made from fresh by using minced beef, then flavouring the meat and shaping them into patties. This is very time-consuming and rarely done in fast food businesses. It is suited only to an establishment that wants to sell the freshest burger. Fast food is about providing quickly prepared foods to the consumer, so for convenience and to minimise preparation times, ready-made frozen burgers are bought in. Although frozen, after they're defrosted, they're still fresh.

Chicken burgers are available as a battered fillet, and small and large sizes are available. You may want to offer a larger-sized chicken burger to create more value for customers. Or you could go for a smaller chicken breast fillet which will be cheaper to stock, but adequate for customer satisfaction. It is also advisable to stock a vegetarian burger to cater for non-meat eaters, although there are not many requests for vegetarian food.

Food items for high profits

A well-kept secret in the trade is that there is a lot of money to be made from the sale of burgers and sausages. They generate more money because they are a lot cheaper to stock than fish. In some areas sausages will sell like hotcakes and they are a favourite with chips.

A sausage dinner, which normally consists of two small sausages, chips, peas and gravy, can be a very good seller in some locations. It is good for profit and the cost of making it is low. The portion of chips is controlled automatically because they are placed in a tray. Peas and gravy sauce are also stocked inexpensively, but are great value for money.

Fishcakes are fairly cheap to produce as they can be made from fish bits and can earn a good profit. They can also be bought frozen. They can be good sellers depending on quality and popularity – this varies from place to place.

Getting the prices right

As fish is expensive, price rises of fish and chips are unavoidable in the future. Supplying fish will cost more and unfortunately the costs may have to be passed on to customers. I think one problem in the industry is that people don't charge enough for fish and chips, which can devalue the product.

Alarm Bell

Charging too little makes it difficult to make a profit unless you sell a lot.

That is why buying a business in an area where prices are low is risky. For a newbie in the business it can be a problem, unlike for some owners who have been running their own businesses for years. They have been committed, worked hard and made their money. If they own the property of their business, its value would have appreciated as well.

There are some owners who run their shops in less expensive areas, where there are economic challenges, but who charge over £4 for fish and chips. Instead of cutting their prices, they concentrate on improving their food quality by using better ingredients plus raising their service. This is good news as that is the point of business – to provide a service and to make a profit. Someone just starting in the trade today must have the prices right to keep themselves in business. If trade is not as good as expected, right pricing can keep them afloat.

Other food supplies

SCAMPI

These small pieces of lobster tail meat are coated in breadcrumbs or batter and deep fried until golden brown. They are best served with tartare sauce. Scampi is a classic that is mostly available in traditional fish and chip outlets. Unfortunately it is expensive to stock and is not a great product for profit. It is also not commonly ordered by customers.

We stock them as we have regular customers who are fans of scampi. Deciding to stock them or not will depend on your outlet and whether you want to keep providing some foods that are not as popular as others, or choose to concentrate fully on other more profitable products such as kebabs and burgers.

KEBABS

Kebabs are made from lamb, beef and chicken meat which is roasted on a vertical rotating spit. Pieces of this marinated meat are placed in pitta bread and served with fresh salad fillings and chilli. The most popular of all kebabs in Europe is the doner kebab. It is the most popular fast food in Germany, sells extremely well in Poland and Romania and is commonly eaten in the UK. They sell well at bar and nightclub closing time.

Kebab meats come in very large pieces and usually come frozen. They are available in sizes from 10lb (4.5kg) to a very large 120lb (54kg). Chicken kebab meat can range from 15lb (6.8kg) to 60lb (27.2kg).

Ready-cooked kebab meat is also available – it comes in sealed tubs which are pre-cooked and frozen. A portion of meat can be heated up in a microwave oven and be ready in three to five minutes. Some will be already cut into slices for ease of use. This method is suited to premises which don't want to invest in expensive kebab equipment.

FRIED CHICKEN

There are quite a few chicken products on the market. Select the one that is suitable for your establishment. The market is competitive so there are new products coming onto it and you may want to stock types that your competitors don't have. If your aim is to provide a multi-food service, selling other products alongside fried fish and chips, then it is logical to source a variety of chicken products.

These products can be chicken breasts, drumsticks or wings. They're delicious and offer a variety of choice when customers feel like having chicken. They come frozen and should be stored in the freezer, and as they can come in quite big pieces they must be defrosted in a microwave before being placed in the chip pan. Chicken nuggets are useful to have on the menu as they are popular with children. They are perfect as part of a kid's meal offer.

PIZZAS

These can be created by using a ready-formed dough and adding toppings – deep pan and thin and crispy bases are available – or you could make the dough from fresh. Sophisticated pizza ovens can cook fresh pizzas in a matter of minutes. The cost of a pizza oven can range from £500 to £1,500 or more.

If pizza is a product you want to add to the business, it must be done properly using professional ovens and equipment. Without the right equipment, a pizza will take some time to cook which means it will take longer to prepare when it is part of a menu or if you're going to deliver it. Also, the correct ingredients and stock must be sourced for pizza making. Do take into account that there are many outlets that have taken on board the pizza concept. They are available frozen and freshly made from supermarkets. Pizzas are easily imitated and reproduced at a high standard.

BANANA FRITTERS

These are quite delicious – simply a banana cut in half, then dipped in batter and fried. They go very well with some golden syrup on top.

SAUCES AND CONDIMENTS

Gravy and **curry** are standard sauces in fish and chip shops, and using the right curry can improve sales. Suppliers that want your business are sometimes able to offer a free bag of sauce mix to sample.

Tomato ketchup is a must and still the nation's favourite sauce. It goes well with chips and burgers. A good **brown sauce** should also be available as some customers prefer it to tomato.

Mayonnaise should be stocked and goes well with beef and chicken burgers.

If the premises has an eat-in area, **tartare sauce** should be stocked as it will be requested by customers to go with fish or scampi.

You should also stock **chilli-based sauces** that suit burgers and kebabs – both a mild and a hot version.

 You don't need to go with well-known household brands – there are other brands that cost less and are very similar in flavour.

PEAS

These are essential with fish and chips for some people. They are cheap to stock and you can find peas that do not require long cooking times.

SALT

The favourite for seasoning and flavouring food. It is sprinkled onto food using a salt shaker that is placed next to the wrapping paper ready to be put on chips. Salt usually come in 10kg bags. Most customers love their salt, but some are aware of the health risks of consuming too much. These customers will usually ask for 'a little bit of salt and plenty of vinegar'.

The health risks of salt

In recent years there has been much concern about the intake of salt in adults and children in the UK as there is strong evidence that a diet high in salt levels is a primary cause of high blood pressure, heart attacks and stomach cancer. There is also evidence that a high intake of salt or salty foods is a cause of obesity, as it causes fluid retention in the body. By reducing salt consumption, the body loses excess water which can result in weight loss. The solution to the health risk of high salt consumption is to provide customers with a healthier alternative. You may want to use salt substitutes that have all the flavour of normal salt, but only one third of the sodium. Losalt and Pansalt are two well-known versions.

VINEGAR

It is essential to have vinegar – along with the salt – to put on fish and chips, kept in a vinegar shaker on the counter. It usually comes in five-litre bottles from the supplier and is diluted with water (the ratio is around one part vinegar to eight parts water). Some come already diluted and ready to use straight out of the bottle.

BEVERAGES

Soft drinks sell well with food and are good for profit. My advice is to stay with the well-known brands as those are usually what customers want. You may want to buy cheaper soft drinks which can increase profits but experience tells me that customers prefer the popular brands. Coca-Cola is a must and also Pepsi-Cola. Customers sometimes refuse to buy Pepsi when Coke is not available – many think that Pepsi is a poor imitation of Coke.

Soft drink companies are clever in their price strategy, as their prices are lower in the winter when people tend to drink fewer cold drinks. They then raise their prices in the summer when the drinks are in demand. As a result it is a good idea to stock more when prices are lower. You should also give people a healthy option such as bottled water. Cartons of juice are also recommended as they are a healthier choice for children.

Non-food supplies

Non-food supplies are things like packaging to keep the food warm and for carrying the food. Deliveries of these will not be as frequently needed as food supplies and depend on how much storage space you have. They are very important and the stock level must be monitored as strictly as food. Without them, you cannot serve people.

You will need the following supplies:

☐ paper: plain paper for wrapping

☐ grease paper: to absorb oil and help in wrapping

☐ cups and lids: to hold sauces

☐ paper bags: to hold sauce cups

☐ plastic forks: to help customers eat their food

☐ trays: to put food on; there are different sizes and types e.g. burger trays, chip trays and so on

☐ carrier bags: for transporting food, with small and larger sizes.

You may want to give some thought to the food trays and carrier bags used as the design and packaging will represent the business. Paying a little more will give you a quality bag with some design. But there is nothing wrong with saving on costs by going cheap and cheerful.

Finding suppliers

The popularity of fast food is booming in the UK and there are many suppliers in this competitive industry. The products from your supplier, as well as the service, should be assessed – and of course their costs.

If you have bought an existing business then you will have access to contacts that are supplying it. It may be logical to stay with suppliers that have provided stock for the business, and then change gradually after you have spent some time running the premises. Or you could make the decision to use entirely new suppliers for stock if you wish. Suppliers can be found online and in the *Yellow Pages*.

ORDERING SUPPLIES

It's important to have a list of suppliers stuck onto a wall or general information board. The person who normally does the ordering may be so used to calling suppliers that they have memorised the numbers. If someone else needs to take over the task they may not have numbers available in their head.

WORKING WITH SUPPLIERS

Let's take fish as an example. Always try to order the freshest fish possible as it will separate you from your competitors. If you receive a fish delivery and the fish does not look fresh enough, do not be afraid to phone your supplier and inform them. By doing this they will know you care about what you are getting and that you will speak up if you find something wrong.

Always remember who is paying who. As a shopkeeper, you are the customer of your suppliers. As it is a competitive industry, you will find that suppliers may even agree to drop some of their prices to get your business. I recently changed to a different potato merchant who offered stock at a reduced price.

HANDLING DELIVERIES

I like to give my suppliers a key to the premises and leave the money for them to collect. There is no waiting around for them. Before this can be done, however, you may want to establish a relationship with them over a period of time to build trust. If you do decide to wait for your deliveries you will have the chance to check both the quality of the stock and that the order is correct.

BUYING FROM A CASH AND CARRY

It makes sense to join a wholesale as there can be some very good deals on beverages and food products. (Certain wholesales allow only business owners to open an account with them.) A good range of beef and chicken burgers can be found at the cash and carry, along with other products. Some wholesalers will even have their own line of catering products which can save costs. Ketchup sauces, relishes and other condiments are available in large containers.

In fact, nearly everything related to the small fast-food outlet can be bought from a cash and carry. There will also usually be regular promotions and special offers on products. When buying stock from a wholesaler it is best to buy everything needed in bulk so that the journey is worthwhile.

 Remember to compare prices from a cash and carry with your normal suppliers, including your transport costs.

I visit the cash and carry once a month mainly to stock up on soft drinks and to purchase some frozen foods. I find that there is a wide range of products and the staff are very helpful as they deal with business owners on a daily basis. There is also a good range of cleaning products that are very good value for money.

USING A SUPERMARKET

You will need to use supermarkets to a certain extent when running a food business. Occasionally, for example, there are some very good deals on soft drinks, such as two-litre bottles.

You can also get cheese to complement burgers, as well as tomatoes, iceberg lettuce, onions and other vegetables. You may find that you visit supermarkets frequently to top up on such items. You can also get good quality baps reasonably inexpensively. I tend to order mine from a local bakery which is situated close to my premises. As I am a loyal customer, I get charged at the wholesale price instead of retail. So by using a local bakery, you may be able to get a reasonable discount.

 When you're short of pies and can't get an order for a couple of days Holland's pies are available in the major supermarkets. Even if you do not stock this brand, they are a good substitute until you get your next delivery.

Summary

Stock must be sourced carefully at the right price and quality. How many products you choose to stock will depend on what kind of establishment you intend to run. If you want to specialise as a fish and chip outlet that provides a wide selection of fish you must focus on sourcing other fish types in addition to commonly-served types like cod and haddock. With fish as your main speciality, you may want to limit burgers and other products so that you can better concentrate your efforts on serving fish. However, you may decide to specialise in burgers and other products as well so that you can cater for a wider clientele.

5
PREPARING FOOD

The information in this chapter is focused mainly on preparing foods and begins by looking at the necessary hygiene practices required in all food businesses.

Understanding the importance of food hygiene

The Food Safety Act 1990 makes you responsible for the food that you sell. Food hygiene legislation affects all food businesses, primary producers (like farmers) and food manufacturers. Most food retailers also need to register with the local authority. UK and European Regulations require all food handlers to be trained in food hygiene.

Food produced should be tasty, provide nutrition and above all be safe to eat. Running a catering outlet, especially if you're going to handle food yourself, requires you to have a valid food safety certificate. Courses are available at colleges or can be studied online and are reasonably inexpensive.

The course will consist of the following:

☐ awareness of the necessity of food safety

☐ personal hygiene

☐ safe cleaning and correct use of chemicals

☐ food safety hazards

☐ temperature control and safe food storage.

Environmental health inspectors (EHOs)

Local authorities have a responsibility to enforce food hygiene laws. Environmental health officers can walk into your premises without notice or appointment, and if they find the conditions of a poor standard, you can be closed down. These officers might visit on a routine inspection, or they might turn up because of a complaint received.

They are allowed to take food samples, request you to put right any problems and stop you from using certain methods in the preparation process. The worst thing that can happen, along with closure of the premises, is that they recommend a prosecution (in very serious cases). If someone gets food poisoning from buying food from your establishment, clearly it will have a negative effect on your reputation.

Inspectors will be glad to give you advice on how to improve your operation so that it complies with their safety regulations. EHOs are trained in their field and can find things that you may have overlooked. EHOs do not visit that often, so when they do pay a visit it is a good opportunity to work with them and ask for their advice.

Food poisoning

Here are some facts about food poisoning:

☐ Thousands of people are known to be affected by food poisoning in the UK, but the real figure is estimated to be around 5.5 million because a lot of cases remain unreported.

☐ Around 60 people die from food poisoning each year.

☐ Food poisoning costs the economy, including employers and our national health service, at least £350 million a year.

☐ 72 per cent of consumers are concerned about hygiene standards in food outlets.

☐ Most consumers who are concerned about hygiene standards in a particular food outlet will not return to buy food there.

☐ 45 per cent of food handlers in food businesses are untrained in food hygiene.

☐ People breaking food safety laws can face fines of up to £20,000 or even imprisonment.

As you can see, the situation is serious. In many establishments, staff are under-trained and some owners are just plain careless. When staff and food handlers have limited knowledge of preparing foods correctly, the product is affected. Businesses in the industry that prepare foods incorrectly can give a bad name to other operators that follow the right procedures.

Be sure to make workers aware of food hygiene and how to prepare food safely. You will thank yourself for doing it and so will your customers.

I have known businesses that have been closed temporarily because of their poor standards in the kitchen. It is important to study fully the practice of correct handling of food and its preparation. Understand the process of every step in food hygiene preparation until your product reaches the customer.

WHAT IS FOOD POISONING AND WHAT CAUSES IT?

Food poisoning is contaminated food that when eaten causes people to vomit, have diarrhoea, stomach pains, headaches or become ill in other ways. It is caused by viruses, toxins or bacteria. A common type of food poisoning in the UK is Salmonella, but the most common type of food poisoning is believed to be caused by a bacteria called Campylobacter. This causes a severe stomach upset – a diarrhoea illness that can last a week or more. The infection usually lasts two to five days, but can be prolonged in adults.

Foods containing unwelcome organisms taste, look and smell like normal edible food which makes it difficult to know if the food is safe to eat just by looking at it. Harmful organisms multiply easily in food, especially in warm and moist conditions. They can spread when food is in contact with contaminated surfaces, preparation areas or kitchen utensils.

Someone who has not washed their hands after using the toilet, or who has been contact with cats and or dogs, will transfer the germs when in contact with food afterwards. Undercooked foods such as meat and eggs are also likely to cause food poisoning. Flies that have contact with food will transfer their germs – and they can carry up to two million bacteria! This can all be avoided with correct practice of food hygiene.

CROSS-CONTAMINATION

Cross-contamination is when bacteria spread between food, surfaces or equipment. It is most likely to happen when raw food touches (or drips onto) cooked foods or has contact with equipment and surfaces.

 Avoid cross-contamination by regularly disinfecting work surfaces and working equipment thoroughly before you start preparing food.

Be sure to thoroughly clean any equipment or area after the preparation of raw food. Make sure that all staff – including you – wash their hands each time they visit the toilet or begin a shift. Staff should come into work clean, and never have a sweaty odour. This is difficult in a food establishment when it can get hot in the premises, but all the more reason to start work clean and fresh. Hair should be washed and never dirty.

THE CONDITIONS REQUIRED FOR BACTERIA GROWTH

The temperature required for bacteria to multiply is 40–145 degrees Fahrenheit. This is the danger zone. Foods need to be cooked above the zone to fully kill bacteria and when you are cooling food make sure its temperature goes below this before being put in the fridge.

Bacteria take very little time to multiply themselves, and in suitable temperatures will grow rapidly. Storing foods in the fridge is crucial to stop bacteria growth as they need moisture and a warm environment. Bacteria cells grow by dividing themselves – one cell of bacteria can transform into millions in only eight hours. Therefore it is absolutely crucial to store foods correctly and to frequently clean surfaces and fridges. This kills germs and prevents contamination.

Observing hygiene

PERSONAL HYGIENE

As well as correct preparation and maintaining clean working areas, personal cleanliness is just as important. Men should be clean shaven, have a short hair cut and appear clean and presentable. Women should have their hair tied back if it's long and also be presented properly. I tend to wear a sports cap when in service, as hair can come off your head and unknowingly land on someone's chips. You could wear one or invest in a catering hat and provide one for all staff. Also, make sure you and your staff wear clean aprons in service.

KEEPING STAFF INFORMED

Staff should be informed of the effects of poor hygiene and what they should do to prevent it. I have found it best to have a short talk to all working staff in a group when they come in for a shift. They respect the seriousness of the issue as everyone is involved. I talk about the need to come into work clean, the importance of hand-washing and of having tidy hair. I also emphasise to them how important it is not to touch their noses or hair especially when customers can see them. This seems to work and most staff are very co-operative.

Alarm Bell

By law, food should not be handled if you or staff are suffering from an illness that is likely to be transmitted through food. Anyone suffering from diarrhoea or vomiting should not return to work until they have had no symptoms for 48 hours.

FIRST AID KIT

The premises needs to have a first aid kit that should have waterproof plasters and bandages. In order to protect food from potential contamination you must provide proper waterproof wound dressings with correct cleansing solutions. The kit should be kept in a waterproof container and be readily available to staff.

In order to limit the possibility of dressings finding their way into food you should use brightly-coloured dressings and wear rubber gloves. You should also avoid the use of needles or safety pins as these may also end up in customers' food.

WASHING HANDS

Effective hand washing must be practised to help prevent harmful bacteria from spreading to food, work surfaces and working equipment. Hands should be washed thoroughly after:

☐ using the toilet

☐ a break

☐ touching raw food

☐ handling food waste or emptying a bin

☐ cleaning.

Here is a thorough six-step method to hand washing which takes just 20 seconds:

1. Rub hands palm to palm.

2. Rub the back of both hands.

3. Clasp fingers together and rub.

4. Rub the finger tips of each hand on the other palm.

5. Rub right thumb clasped in left hand, and then the opposite, plus wrists.

6. Rub finger nails on each palm, left then right.

When you have finished, rinse the soap off your hands with warm water and dry your hands thoroughly with a clean towel.

TOP TEN POINTS OF FOOD HYGIENE

1. Wash your hands thoroughly before any contact with food.

2. Do not place raw food next to cooked food. It can cross-contaminate.

3. Do not store cleaning chemicals and disinfectants close to areas where food is placed.

4. Wash your hands after contact with raw meat.

5. Always wash the chopping board and knife after using them with raw meat.

6. Make sure work areas are clean.

7. Always make sure food is cooked all the way through and is served piping hot.

8. Avoid habits, like touching your nose, mouth and hair, when handling food.

9. If you receive deliveries, inspect them for freshness.

10. Make sure that you are clean and tidy before the beginning of a shift.

SMOKING

Smoking inside all public places has been banned, including all pubs, restaurants and food outlets. It makes it safe for other people and workers and it supports food hygiene. At no time should anyone smoke inside the premises. It is a serious offence. All staff who smoke should go outside the building. When they come back from their break, they must wash their hands.

Storing food

Storing food properly is an important part of reducing the risks of food poisoning. Some foods, such as pies or vegetables, must be stored in the fridge and eaten within a short space of time. Chilling food properly helps to stop harmful bacteria from growing. Other types of food that need to be kept in the fridge are those with a use-by date, cooked food and salads. It is very important not to leave these types of food standing around at room temperature. Put food that needs to be kept chilled in the fridge straightaway.

Other foods, such as batter mix and canned foods can last a longer period of time and be stored at room temperature. After opening dried foods like batter mix reseal them tightly. It is important also to store cooking utensils in cupboards and drawers to prevent contamination. These storage spaces should be cleaned regularly.

PRE-PACKED FOODS

Most pre-packed foods will carry either a use-by or best-before date. Foods that carry use-by dates are spoiled more easily than those that have a best-before date, which have a longer life. It can be dangerous to eat foods past their useable date, so any foods past their shelf life must be thrown away. If foods are within their useable dates but look or smell bad, it is best to throw them away.

Alarm Bell

Frozen stock must be monitored carefully as less popular items can be easily forgotten.

As frozen items contain ice, care must be taken to cook them properly. Large frozen items can be defrosted in a microwave for two to three minutes so that they can be cooked more easily.

IMPLEMENTING HACCP PRINCIPLES

HACCP (hazard analysis critical point) aims to reduce risks and to control hazards in the food preparation process. Introduced by the European parliament, the HACCP principles became part of food hygiene law in the UK from 1 January 2006 and have been made part of food safety legislation in many other countries. (The principles were originally developed by the Pillsbury company and NASA in the 1960s to guarantee the safety of food made for astronauts.)

The principles involve having a close look at what you do in your business and what could go wrong. A key part is identifying the 'critical control points' – the places you need to focus on to prevent hazards or to reduce risks. Procedures must then be put in place to make sure hazards are controlled and what action needs to be taken if something does go wrong. You need to make sure that your procedures are working and record this on paper to demonstrate that the controls are successful.

Some people think that using HACCP is a very complicated process, but it is actually relatively easy to follow. The main thing is to have the right procedures that are appropriate for your business. You can develop your own procedures based on the principles of HACCP.

For convenience, a comprehensive pack has been introduced by the Food Standards Agency to help food businesses implement HACCP. Once the pack has been completed, filling in the diary takes only about two minutes a day. If an environmental health inspector looks at the premises, the diary can give him or her a clear view of the safety of food sold, instead of just going on the clean working display of the premises.

For more information on HACCP go to www.food.gov.uk.

Cooking foods

You will be responsible for all the food you sell being cooked properly. Cooking or reheating foods correctly kills any harmful bacteria, so it is extremely important to make sure that food is piping hot all the way through. You must make sure that products made from minced meat, such as pies, burgers and sausages, are cooked thoroughly because bacteria can lurk in the middle of them.

As mentioned previously, frozen items contain ice and can be more difficult to cook. If they are not cooked thoroughly they may contain bacteria which will be likely to cause food poisoning.

Disposing of food waste

You must have facilities in place for storing and disposing of food waste and other rubbish. Bins should be removed regularly to avoid a build up. You must put food waste and other rubbish in containers that can be closed, unless you can satisfy your local authority that other types of containers or systems of disposing of waste are appropriate. These containers must be easy to clean and in good condition.

Be sure to wash your hands when touching bins after emptying them. There is a lot of bacteria in those areas that can get onto your hands and then be transferred to food. Also be sure to keep bins away from raw and cooked foods.

Cleaning

Cleaning gets rid of bacteria on equipment and working surfaces, and it helps to stop harmful bacteria from spreading onto food. Regular cleaning is needed to keep premises fresh and germ-free.

Apart from preparing and cooking somebody's food, a lot of cleaning must be done to maintain hygiene standards. Customers notice a premises that isn't clean. When a premises appears unhygienic, it gives the impression that the food is unclean and unsafe to eat. Regular cleaning must be done to keep the premises looking respectable for your customers.

Alarm Bell

People sometimes forget or do not realise that cleaning is a big part of running a catering business and needs to done daily.

You need to maintain a clean premises because:

☐ it makes a good first impression

☐ it reduces the risk of food contamination

☐ it lets the staff know that the owners take the business seriously and also want them to work in a clean environment

☐ customers and staff will spread the word about how spotless and clean the premises is

☐ it gives a good impression to an environmental health inspector if they visit the premises.

The premises should be clean prior to opening. When you have closed for the day the work doesn't end, as there is more cleaning.

At the end of the day:

☐ wash the working utensils

☐ clean the fryer thoroughly

☐ take apart and wash the chipper and any other main working equipment

☐ hose down the potato preparation area

☐ sweep and mop all the floors of the premises

☐ clean the fridge to get rid of any germs in order to keep food fresh.

Cleaning thoroughly can take half an hour to 45 minutes depending on the speed and quality of your cleaning. This does not include general cleaning maintenance of the shop when you're open and there are quiet intervals. So you see there are plenty of jobs to do in a catering business.

I like to do a big cleaning session where each member of staff is involved at the end of the working week. The whole premises and its equipment are cleaned from top to bottom. Fridges and freezers are cleaned out thoroughly, and moved out from their places which are then swept and mopped. The kitchen and shop area must be spotless. If you do this when you start the week there is clean, tidy environment to work in.

Summary

Being aware of basic food hygiene is fundamental in the preparing of food. Your food must be safe to eat. Cleaning regularly will ensure hygienic surroundings for customers and staff. All areas of hygiene must be taken seriously such as no smoking, cooking foods and washing hands. Practising correct food hygiene will raise the standards of your quality and service. Also, you will be likely to pass the standards expected from an environmental health inspector.

6
FOOD PREPARATION

Food must be prepared properly before it gets sold. Correct food preparation will raise service standards, and thoroughly preparing your foods using the right procedures will increase their quality.

Preparing potatoes

Potatoes need to be rumbled in the potato peeler which will take around two minutes when the peeler is filled. Once they are peeled, they must be kept in a large container and preserved with fresh water. Water will also stop them from changing colour.

Potatoes usually need some tidying up with a knife to remove some inedible parts before chipping. The potatoes will vary in size and some may be larger than others, in which case they must be cut into two to make it easier to chip them.

There are some varieties of potatoes which don't require much or any work. Potato merchants will usually inform you if they have these potatoes and the fact that they don't need much work would usually be reflected in the price.

Alarm Bell

Sharpen the knife from time to time but be very careful as it is not uncommon to cut your finger.

Potatoes should be prepared early before an opening. How many get rumbled will depend on the business of the outlet, but calculate what you need because rumbling too many may leave too many left over after a shift. Since they can be preserved in water they can be used the following day but it is best to keep this to a minimum as potatoes from the day before will not be as fresh. More potatoes will usually be needed on busier days such as Friday and Saturday.

Alarm Bell

Do not attend to something else when you're rumbling potatoes because when they are left in the peeler for too long their size reduces. They will cut fewer chips and you will lose profit.

KEEPING POTATOES FRESH

☐ Fresh tap water will preserve and maintain potatoes and they can be left in it overnight.

☐ Storing potatoes for more than two days will have an effect on their freshness, flavour and reliability to fry well.

☐ Potatoes contain sugar content causing them to change colour. To prevent this, dry-white can be used to prevent discolouration.

☐ In the summer, because of higher temperatures, potatoes are difficult to keep fresh. Avoid having too many left over after the evening shift.

☐ Potatoes need to be stored at 7-10°C (45-50°F), preferably in a dark and airy space.

MAKING CHIPS

☐ Rumble the potatoes.

☐ Use a knife to tidy them and cut larger-sized ones in half.

☐ Put some in a chipper to cut them or hand cut them for a bigger-size chip.

☐ Throw some in a hot pan to fry.

☐ Cook for around six to eight minutes or until golden brown.

Preparing fish

Commonly-used fish like haddock will usually come in a stone of 45 fillets which are already skinned and boned. These require minimal work and only need to be checked quickly prior to frying. (You can of course prepare them earlier.) Some bones may be present – how many will depend upon whoever did the boning earlier.

Cut the end (tail) off a fillet because it is smaller than the rest of the fish, which means it cooks more quickly and gives a burnt taste. This can also be done when you are preparing earlier. A solution to this is simply to fold the tail over before frying.

Larger-sized fillets can be split into two, but will need to be skinned and boned properly. A fish knife is ideal to do this – it normally has a long blade, or any blade that is long and flat. Always sharpen well before use.

TECHNIQUE WHEN PREPARING LARGER FILLETS

White sea-fish like haddock and cod are big and the skinning and filleting takes more time. Fish that come whole require much more work. When working on a whole fish, decide on the size of each fillet. Then cut portions of the fish, and skin and bone them using the technique below.

Hold the fish vertically by the tail.

☐ Make a small cut at the end of the tail.

☐ Press and slide the blade away from you whilst pulling with the hand on the tail towards you. Take the skin off but avoid the flesh as much as you can.

☐ Once the skin has come off, lay the fillet down and separate it with the knife into two similar-sized fillets. To do this, cut the fillet with a diagonal stroke.

☐ Check for bones in both fillets and remove them taking as little flesh as possible.

FILLETING FISH

If you introduce different types of fish to the menu, many may not be available as ready-prepared fillets because demand for them as fillets are low. Although fishmongers can fillet them for you, being in the trade you should know how to properly fillet a fish. You will need a cutting board or a flat surface for all your preparation and a sharp flat blade for cutting along the back bone.

☐ Using a sharp knife, make a cut just before the gills and slice down to the bone.

☐ Without moving the blade, turn it and slice right across (diagonally) close to the backbone through to the tail, until the fillet has come away from the rest of the fish. Be sure to slice close to the bone so that no meat is wasted.

☐ Turn the fish over and repeat the process on the other side.

☐ The skin will now need to be separated from the fillet (as above).

Making the perfect batter

Batter is essential for fish frying and can often be overlooked in terms of quality, but it is important as it is eaten with the fish. It's a good idea to try out a few fish batters from suppliers instead of sticking with the first one you use.

Batter can be prepared manually using a whisk or alternatively with an electric mixer. Making batter manually can be more convenient as an appliance requires cleaning afterwards.

The batter should be the right thickness and consistency to fry fish correctly. The best fried fish is when it has a layer of batter on it which is not too thick and not too thin. The fish can be ruined if the batter is not right.

Batter insulates the fish from the heat of the fryer, and, if required goes golden brown. A water-based batter will take some time to brown fish because the water has to evaporate before it will cook. Adding some vodka will make it evaporate much more quickly. It is a fine art making batter – and we haven't even covered frying yet.

Some people like the fish batter bits known as 'scraps' which are collected each time the pan is sieved. When scraps are asked for it is free of charge.

Some guidelines on batter:

☐ Try not to make batter too watery; the fish will appear small as the batter will be unable to stick well.

☐ Batter sticks to the fish, but putting some corn starch on both sides of the fish before dipping in batter will help to create fewer bits in the pan.

☐ Batter should be placed in the fridge for 30 minutes before being used.

☐ Do not leave any left-over batter to sell the next day as it will be flat.

☐ Adding beer to the batter will increase its crunchiness.

SIMPLE BATTER RECIPE

☐ 1 cup strong flour

☐ 1½ cups cold water

☐ Pinch of salt

☐ 1 tsp of vinegar

☐ 1 tsp of bicarbonate of soda

Put the flour in a bowl, then add the cold water, the salt, and mix to an appropriate consistency.

Add the vinegar and bicarbonate of soda, then mix well.

Keep the mixture refrigerated until you need it.

BEER BATTER RECIPE

- ☐ 1 cup flour
- ☐ 1 egg, beaten
- ☐ 1 tsp garlic powder
- ☐ ½ tsp ground black pepper
- ☐ 1½ cups beer

Mix the flour, egg, garlic powder, and black pepper.

Stir in the beer (you can add more than one cup to create the desired texture). The more the beer is cooked and reduced, the stronger the flavour will be.

PREPARING A BOUGHT MIX

Add cold water (the amount will vary depending how much mix you are using). It should be four parts batter mix to around five parts water, depending on how thick you want the mixture to be.

Add a little salt.

Mix it using a whisk to the right consistency – not too thick but not thin either.

 Try not to over-mix batter as it can become flat.

Preparing sauces

The most common sauces in a traditional fish and chip business are gravy and curry. Most of them come in a concentrated powder and no further flavouring is needed. The nature of the business is to provide fast food and sauces do not take long to make – a pot of gravy can be made in as little as five minutes using boiling water from the kettle.

There are many gravy brands available and they are similar in flavour. Customers do not seem to be too choosy over gravy as long it is a reasonable standard. This is a little different for curry. A traditional chip-shop curry sauce may not be suited to everyone's taste as it is quite bland. Many people like other curries that provide more spice and flavour.

MAKING GRAVY AND CURRY SAUCE FROM POWDER

☐ Heat some water in a saucepan.

☐ Put some gravy/curry mix in a small bowl. Add a small amount of the warm water and stir to create a smooth paste.

☐ Pour the mixture into the hot water and stir well.

☐ Let the mixture heat up and start to simmer.

☐ When simmering, check the thickness. Add more hot water if it's too thick; if it's too thin add more mixture.

Some curry sauces come as a solid paste. These need to be transferred into a pan of hot water and stirred. Allow time to bubble and add more curry paste to make the sauce the right thickness.

Of course it is possible to make your own sauces, but for convenience these ready-made sauces speed up preparation time and allow you time to focus on other aspects of preparation.

Preparing peas

Chippy peas are dry and need to be soaked in cold water for a minimum of 12 hours, preferable overnight. Add some bicarbonate of soda before putting them in cold water – this speeds up the process of softening them.

When they have been soaked:

☐ Drain them and give them a rinse under the tap, then transfer them to a pot.

☐ Add hot water from the kettle and fill the pot, covering all the peas. Add a few drops of green colouring.

☐ Cook on a medium heat for just over an hour (depending on the amount of peas).

☐ Check them regularly and add more water if needed.

☐ Cook longer for a mushy result.

 It is always best to be prepared with peas as they need to be soaked before they can be cooked. You do not want to run out of peas during an opening.

Making fishcakes

Making your own fishcakes will result in a fresher product than if you buy them frozen, but it will take more preparation time.

METHOD 1

☐ Boil and mash some potatoes and add fish bits.

☐ Add salt and pepper. (I like to add stuffing as well for more flavour.)

☐ Make them into similar sized burger-shaped potato cakes.

☐ Dip in batter and fry until cooked or golden brown.

METHOD 2

☐ Cut two oval shaped slices of potato and place some fish between them.

☐ Dip in batter and fry until potato is cooked through and golden brown.

Making potato cakes

I tend to makes these only when a customer requests it. They are round thin slices of potato, dipped in batter and deep fried. When slicing them, try to cut them as thin as you can to reduce the cooking time. Be sure to give them enough frying time because their size is bigger than chips, so be patient as they can take a little longer to cook. Aim for a golden brown effect.

Preparing kebabs

Too many shops have kebabs that don't taste good. Be sure to stock only the best quality kebab meat available. Test the different meats then stay with one supplier when the standard is acceptable. Have both medium and large sizes of kebabs available; you may also want to offer a mixed-meat kebab which has all the meats in one. Select good quality chilli sauces to complement them – preferably a mild and hot version.

☐ Depending on what type of kebab grill you use, the meat will generally be ready to be carved in around 30-45 minutes. Be sure not to over cook the meat as the top and bottom edges will be difficult to cut.

☐ The meat is cut with a sharp electric knife and no other substitute blade should be used.

☐ Warm the kebab bun up in any domestic toaster. It can be filled with lots of fresh salad depending what the customer asks for.

Making pizzas

Dough bases are available in different sizes and can bought ready-formed so they only need defrosting (Making the dough fresh is very time consuming.) Toppings are placed on the dough and the pizza can be made in five to eight minutes using a specialised oven. Some advanced pizza-making ovens can make a good standard pizza in under five minutes.

You will need to decide whether you want to buy the toppings frozen or fresh. It is a good idea to serve a range of pizzas, including a vegetarian version, although normally only two or three types sell well. They should be available in different sizes with deep pan or thin crust bases. With the right equipment, pizzas are quite simple to produce.

Preparing burgers

It is quite straightforward to cook and serve burgers. Cook the burger and put it in a bun with cheese, salad and sauce. However you may want to serve your burgers differently to create an edge on your competitors. Onions can be caramelised, and tomatoes fried in a pan will give burgers a special touch and a much more distinct flavour. A variety of cheeses can be provided and melted on burgers.

It is also a good idea to offer a blend of salads. Pan-fried red or green peppers and thinly-sliced carrots work well. Simpler salad combinations like onions and lettuce and tomatoes are often what people want on a burger.

To stand out from the competition, have a diverse range of toppings. Crispy bacon, honey-cured ham, cooked fresh chillies and jalapenos are just some of the toppings that can be served. Some catering businesses that specialise in burgers have their own secret sauce. You don't need to go to such lengths as many supermarkets stock interesting condiments and relishes. But you can make your own if you have a good recipe.

Many customers like their chicken burgers simply with mayonnaise and some iceberg lettuce.

If you plan to offer burgers in different sizes, such as a quarter pounder or half pounder, be sure to display them on your menu. You may want to name your burgers to add individuality. For example extra large burgers can be given names such as 'king size double cheese burgers' or 'monster burgers'. This adds identity to your products.

Some customers request what we call a 'fish burger', which is fried fish put in a bun. They are popular during lunch openings but not often asked for during the evening.

I try to offer a range of burgers to the customer and also try to introduce different toppings. You may want to spend some time creating burgers that will appeal to your local market. Remember, however, that although being creative is beneficial to the business, you also need to give the customer what they want. They may prefer a simple burger with some salad and ketchup.

Tailor the product to your market and style of establishment.

Preparing for an opening

Work is done behind the scenes before the premises opens. Everything needs to be ready prior to opening so that all that is left to do is to wait for staff to arrive and a customer to walk in. You may want your staff to come in before opening time and help in the preparation. In a husband and wife partnership, each can take turns in preparing before an opening, or both can prepare together to lessen the work and increase the speed.

I can't stress enough that preparing thoroughly is the key to preventing any unnecessary mistakes. Preparing is best done at least an hour before an opening. Remember that a customer can walk in the minute you turn the sign from closed to open, so early preparation will avoid customers having to wait or being disappointed. Being on the ball is important in a fast-food business which requires exactly what it says – fast-prepared foods.

 Preparing thoroughly before an opening guarantees efficiency and speeds up the delivery of food to customers.

If, for example, steak and kidney puddings have not been placed in the steamer, a customer cannot have one if they order it. Perhaps you ran out of salad but didn't replenish the stock; as a result a customer is unable to have it with their burger. People are usually in a hurry these days and most do not like to wait. Once the shop is open for business, all the products need to be available to the customer.

You will have to decide how long you need to spend preparing for an opening. I find that to be very thorough, it can take at least 45 minutes to get everything ready. This includes some general cleaning duties. It's not possible always to predict what items you'll need during a shift, but in the trade, all the products on the menu should be available to the consumer.

BEFORE AN OPENING

☐ Rumble enough potatoes for the day and chip some for frying.

☐ Prepare sauces and peas and place them in the bain-marie to keep them hot.

☐ Make the batter.

☐ Turn on fryer/other main equipment.

☐ Butter some buns or baps for display.

☐ Prepare some salads to put on burgers.

☐ Heat up pies and place them for display and place puddings in the steamer.

☐ Prepare kebab meat.

☐ Take fish out of the fridge.

☐ Make sure the shop area is clean and tidy.

☐ Be sure the salt and vinegar shakers are full as well as other condiments like ketchup sauces.

☐ Sieve out pans and throw a batch of chips into the pan.

☐ Cook sausages and other food items and display them.

☐ Before opening, fry some fish and place in the display cabinet.

After an opening

When you have closed, apart from doing general cleaning, be sure that all the equipment is turned off. It is also the time to prepare for the next opening. If you have closed for the day, you will need to monitor and order any stock required. Refer to your timetable or what you need to monitor on that particular day.

Spending some time after service seeing what needs to be done – such as cleaning duties and stock monitoring – is important. You need to be very thorough as the quality of your service has a lot to do with how much time is spent in the business behind the scenes. You can also spend time reflecting on the performance in service and of staff to see what can be improved.

 If any stock needs to be replenished, be sure to write a list of what needs to be ordered.

GENERAL THINGS TO DO AFTER A LUNCH OPENING

☐ Have a look at the level of potatoes left. If needed rumble some and tidy them with a knife.

☐ Check the fish and if needed prepare some for the next service.

☐ Have a look at the level of gravy, curry and peas.

☐ If there is a low level of batter left, it will need to be topped up.

☐ Check on other food types.

☐ Check stock levels generally.

What is done after an opening can determine how prepared you are for the next shift.

Checking stock

It is extremely important for the food stock to be rotated correctly as the old should be used before the new and not the other way round. Careless monitoring will cause new stock to be used and the old will be left to go off.

Stock rotation is done when a stock delivery is received and through the working day. Remember that older stock must go first – negligence in using the wrong stock will drastically affect standards. If you find stock that is not so fresh it must be thrown away.

Alarm Bell

Correct stock rotation avoids any careless mistakes and ensures the food is fresh.

Care should be taken to monitor stock levels, preferably on a daily basis. Go through the fridges every morning and see which stock must be used – some food may not be suitable for sale the next day. It does not take much for a mistake to happen. Nothing is worse than a customer bringing food back to say it is off. Monitoring stock and its freshness should never be overlooked.

It helps to have a notebook and create a list of your items. Mark the stock that needs to be replenished and tick off the items that do not need an order. It does take some skill to monitor stock levels and order the right amounts. Overloading with too much stock will waste storage space. Try to get the hang of ordering and keeping in the right amounts so that products are available for customers and the space available is well utilised.

Summary

It is vital to prepare foods well. Both fish and potatoes need plenty of time to be prepared. How long fish will take to prepare depends on which fish types you use and how well your fishmonger prepares them. Remember, there must be no bones in any of the fish. Customers could choke or hurt their mouth while chewing on fish containing bones. It is your job to see that each fish remains bone-free before it is fried. The work done before and after an opening will play an important part in the success of the operation.

7
THE ART OF FRYING

Frying is a unique method of cooking as it seals in flavour. Although it is somewhat underrated in the general catering industry, fried food has its own characteristic flavour. It is fast – most food can be fried in around five minutes. The short cooking time needed means that food can be prepared when required.

Shallow frying

This method of frying is cooking food in shallow oil. The results are quite different from food produced by deeper oil levels. Since the oil level is low, it heats up much more quickly and food is produced faster. There is also a difference in the food's flavour – it gives food a unique crispy taste.

Shops that shallow fry do so because it generates a different flavour from the conventional method. With smaller amounts of oil, which heat up easily, the food is more vulnerable to being burned. But it is ideal to create good flavours that are distinct from the usual method.

Advantages: Quicker cooking times and unique taste. Oil reheats faster to frying temperature.

Disadvantages: Fat needs to be added frequently. Limited frying volumes.

Deep-fat frying

This is the usual way to fry food, and is the most common form of frying used in fast-food businesses. The chip pan is filled to around just over half its capacity. There is no need to top up fat all the time. Most shops fry like this, mainly for the large capacity and the fact that you don't have to constantly top up fat as for shallow frying.

Advantages: Efficient, will fry large volumes, e.g chips. Can create good standards of food.

Disadvantages: Oil is heated more slowly, so it is more difficult to brown and crisp food.

Using the right frying fat

Beef dripping was used in early fish and chip shops but is unsuitable today, especially for vegetarians and people who do not eat beef. There is a wide range of brands and types available, and you should choose one that's reliable and cost effective.

The cost of all frying fat has gone up so it is important to choose wisely looking at cost and quality. Try not to get used to one type of medium or brand. Using good quality vegetable fat will save money as it will last longer and is more efficient than a cheaper one. If you use a cheaper alternative, the fat will burn more quickly which will increase your costs.

It is more economical to use fat in a modern frying range than an older version because they tend to be more efficient. Selecting the right fat as well can also make a substantial difference to costs. This is even more true when using older range versions. It is also makes for better-tasting food since food absorbs some of the oil/fat.

Types of fat

Vegetable fat: Most do not contain hydrogenated fat which has high levels of trans-fatty acids and poses a health concern. They are usually pure vegetable. Most contain just a fraction of trans-fatty acids.

Palm oil: This is good for frying. It doesn't need hydrogenation which means it does not have trans-fatty acids. The oil comes from the fruit of a palm tree.

Beef dripping: Modern versions of this traditional frying medium come processed, are very efficient, and give food a strong likeable flavour. However, it is not suited to people such as vegetarians and those with certain faiths.

Lard: This, made from purified pork fat, was once used by many cooks. Now it has been replaced by vegetable fats because of its high saturated fat content.

Groundnut oil: This oil is made from peanuts. Some shop owners use it for its unique flavour.

Rapeseed oil: Made from a yellow flowering plant (Brassica napus), it is sometimes compared with olive oil for its nutritional value. It is a healthy heart oil as it contains omega-6 and omega-3 acids.

SOLID FATS

Solid frying fats have to be taken out of the carton and melted down gently at temperatures not exceeding 132°C (270°F) before heating to frying temperature. If this procedure is not followed, the frying life can be reduced.

It is best to empty the fat into the pan before the range is switched on to avoid any chances of scalding, or you can shuffle small portions into the pan instead of topping it up with a full block.

LIQUID OILS

Liquid oils are easier to handle and more convenient to use because they can be poured so they do not need to be melted in order to be used. Since oil is not solid, it is easily transferred into the pan. However, transporting and storing oil is not as easy as solid fats which come in a box.

Fat absorption from foods

When cooking foods, whether deep-fat frying or shallow frying, you will need to top up the fat as it will burn and the food will absorb some of the fat. Chips absorb five to six per cent – this means that 10 kg of potatoes will pick up about 500-600g of fat during frying. Fat absorption will also depend upon frying times: the longer the frying period, the greater the absorption.

Keep in mind that the lower the temperature, the greater the absorption, so the pan must be kept at an appropriate temperature before any food is put in. When cooking frozen foods the fat temperatures can drop by 18-28°C when the food is placed in the hot oil. To save the oil used, foods should be drained well and the tray that collects fat from the chip-box should be put back into the pan.

Preparing foods for frying

Foods should be as dry as possible before frying. Potatoes especially tend to make the oil bubble, so be sure to drain enough excess water from potatoes before chipping them. If not the oil will froth a lot and burn more slowly. Remember that potatoes also discolour if they are prepared in advance.

Large frozen food pieces should be defrosted first to remove ice, and any excess water should be discarded before frying. Fragile foods must be handled carefully so they don't break up during the frying process as charred particles that break away will gather at the bottom of the pan.

Never add salt to food before frying, ideally not even in batter. If there is an accumulation of salt in the pan, it will speed up the deterioration process of the oil.

GENERAL GUIDELINES FOR FRYING

☐ Remember to sieve out the pans before frying.

☐ Always make sure the oil is hot. If it is not hot enough, the food will not fry, or fry too slowly.

☐ The heat must be controlled so you don't burn the chips.

☐ Top up oil when needed. When you're using fresh fat, the food will look and taste better.

☐ When taking chips and other foods out of the pan, give them a good shake and let the oil drain as foods will have absorbed some fat.

Frying fish

Fish has some water content, and depending on the temperature of your fridge, it may even carry some ice. During an opening, some fish should be taken out the fridge ready for frying. If you put fish straight from the fridge into the fryer it will take longer to cook because of its temperature.

When the heat of the oil is above 191°C (375°F), the oil will burn more quickly and if fish is fried at too high a temperature the batter will cook faster and will become too hard. This means the meat at the centre of the fish may be uncooked. If the temperature is too low, fast absorption will be greater and the fish and batter will be soft, having no crisp.

Remember that white fish does not take long to cook – it can be ready in as little as two and a half minutes per side in hot oil which gives an overall time of five minutes. You know it is ready when the batter is fairly crispy. Denser fish like salmon takes longer to cook at around ten minutes.

If you are going to have a large fish on your menu, be sure to give it a longer frying time. Large fish is half a fish, or a smaller piece and a normal fish put together to create a larger fish. It is then dipped in batter and when placed in the pan the two pieces stick together.

 A number of fried fish should be ready on display to avoid customers waiting; as people walk in they tend to have what is ready.

Fish frying takes some skill – it is not as simple as throwing in other foods like burger and chicken. Fish needs to be dipped in batter first, then put in the pan evenly and flat on one side. The temperature of the oil must be hot enough or the fish may curl. Make sure that both sides of the fish get enough frying time. You can also press down on the fish for 15-20 seconds with the frying tool to make sure the fish gets thoroughly cooked.

It is not usual to flavour fish before frying as the batter used will have some salt in it, but I have found that adding some flavour to the fillets before battering them means they are tastier. You can choose to add a touch of salt and pepper, or other flavours to the fillets, prior to frying. Or you could leave them untouched and let the salt and vinegar shakers enhance the flavour after cooking.

HOW TO MAKE A LIGHTLY-BATTERED FISH

A lot of customers will ask for a lightly-battered fish as they may not like batter, or prefer just a little batter. It is difficult to fry a fish without any batter on it as the batter keeps the fish together when cooked in oil.

To cook fish with a little batter, you must coat the whole fillet with batter, then try to wipe as much as you can off one side of the fillet. The fish with the side that has batter on should be placed in the oil first. Another way is to dip the fish in batter then wipe just a little off both sides before cooking it. I prefer the first method in which one side of the fish is crispy and other side, the white flesh of the fish, is seen.

Chip frying

The nature of a fast-food business is to produce food quickly. This means it is not always possible to make chips from fresh which can take around six to eight minutes. The time it takes can also differ depending on the volume of chips put in the pan. The more chips there are, the longer it takes.

Many customers do not want to wait. To make chips more quickly you can prepare them earlier by par-frying or blanching them to speed up the cooking process. If a customer asks for fully fresh chips they should get what they request. Chips are still fresh if they have been par-fried. Par-frying means taking chips out when they're half cooked – when they change a little in colour or when they start to get soft. When the chips are needed put them back in the pan and take them out when golden brown.

BLANCHING

You can follow these guidelines for blanching chips. Blanch them at 168-177°C (30-350°F) until almost cooked, but not brown. After draining they can be stored, but should be refrigerated for no more than two hours. Chips that have been already blanched will brown at 191°C (375°F) after two to three minutes.

Cooking chips from fresh without blanching them first is tricky but can be done. You must ensure that the chips are cooked thoroughly because if they are under-cooked the customer will not be pleased. Two pans must be used to keep up with the speed and demand of producing chips from fresh.

Alarm Bell

It takes skill to be able to make fresh chips for each customer, especially at busy periods when there is a queue of people waiting to get served.

I try to deliver fresh chips as often as I can, though I do blanch a small amount just in case they are needed. Cooking chips straight through is done at 188-191°C (370-375°F) until brown and cooked for around six to eight minutes. I find that the customer appreciates freshly-made chips and we receive frequent compliments from customers. Also, we choose to shallow fry so that chips cook more quickly and are crispier. You will need to choose the method that suits your establishment.

Cooking frozen food

Frozen foods carry some water content, which produces steam during frying. Large thick pieces of frozen food are difficult to cook right through and they reduce the temperature of the oil. As long as the piece of food is small, this may not be a problem, but larger pieces benefit from thawing before frying. In this case, be sure to drain the defrosted food to remove excess moisture produced by the melting ice. Defrosted items of food also need to be handled carefully, because they are often fragile.

BURGERS

Burgers are generally very easy to cook. As they are small thin patties of beef they are normally quicker to cook than fish. Be sure to cook burgers all the way through and not to leave any pink bits in the middle; don't overcook them either – be sure to know their exact cooking times. The burgers should be flipped over so that both sides are cooked.

CHICKEN

Chicken pieces that are large should be left to cook longer than fish. They must also be turned regularly so that they are cooked properly. Large chicken pieces will take about five minutes of frying time but only when they have been defrosted a little in the microwave.

SMALLER ITEMS

Smaller items like chicken nuggets, scampi or frozen fishcakes cook fairly quickly, taking a little less time because of their size. In fact you should be careful not to overcook them as they can end up too brown and dry.

SAUSAGES

Sausages are an easy item to cook, although they need to be cooked thoroughly. When ready they will float on the surface of the oil and sizzle. Allow around three minutes of sizzling time and turn them occasionally. But try not to overcook them or split them – they are a general item which is always available in display cabinets, unlike other items that are usually prepared when asked for. The perfectly cooked sausage is one which has a nice colour, not too brown, and is succulent and juicy when eaten.

Using two or more pans

Most of the time you will have two pans operating – one for frying chips and the other for cooking fish, burgers and other food items. It takes practice to watch two pans; when chips have been thrown into one pan and covered, to it can be quite easy to forget them which can lead to them burning and other food being overcooked.

Alarm Bell

You need good reflexes to move from pan to pan and produce good food.

Some ranges have three pans. They are useful in busy periods – two pans can be used to fry chips leaving one pan to cook other foods. Using three pans simultaneously requires skill and you need to be very alert. Once you are able to manage the frying, you may find that you're the only one able to do it. It's a good idea to train someone else too so that they can take your place when necessary.

USING ONE CHIP PAN

Using one pan for cooking will save on gas usage. You can do this when there is a quiet period in the business or perhaps when the lunch opening does not need both chip pans. It takes some practice to use one pan, as you are cooking chips, fish and other foods, so it can get overcrowded.

It is difficult if an opening suddenly becomes busy as it takes some time for a second pan to be ready for operation. The best way to handle one pan is that if chips are needed, they should be the priority. However, if the oil is hot and you need to fry several fish it makes sense to place the fish in first as they take a shorter time to cook. After they are done, the chips can be thrown in immediately.

Here are my tips for frying:

☐ Use two pans in busy openings to ensure efficiency and a reliable service.

☐ Be aware of all the pans in operation and don't just focus on what's cooking in one pan.

☐ Top up pans with fresh fat when needed.

☐ Control the heat on all pans so that none of them overheats.

☐ Know the cooking times of foods and don't rely on guess work.

Safety precautions when frying

Chip pan fires cause the most casualties in house fires. Accidents also happen in many fast-food businesses so it is important to be aware of the problem. Shops have burnt to the ground or been badly damaged due to careless mistakes working with oil.

Using oil in frying is a potential hazard. When oil is heated over its limit it burns, smokes and even ignites and bursts into flames. Chip pan fires start when oil overheats, then catches fire. They can also start when wet chips are placed in hot oil making it bubble which can cause it to overflow. The design of a frying range doesn't mean it can't catch fire.

People get hurt and even die from chip pan fires so it is a very serious problem.

Alarm Bell

Oil that is overheated can ignite spontaneously – it does not need to have contact with a flame.

PREVENTING FIRES

Fires often happen because a thermostat on a range has been left unattended. They can also be caused by the frying medium frothing over because of the continued use of wet or frozen food. The range should never be left without supervision for more than ten seconds, and the pan must be controlled so it does not overheat.

If the oil is too hot, turn it down and give it time to cool. When a pan has started smoking do not throw chips or any food in until it has had time to reduce its temperature. Never turn your attention away from the pan.

WHAT TO DO IF THERE IS A CHIP PAN FIRE

Call the fire service immediately and keep all the staff and other people in the shop away from the pan. Have a large towel handy (do not wet it) then try and put it over the pan. The premises should have a fire blanket which has been designed to stop a fire – use it and leave it in position for a minimum of 20 minutes as this will make sure that the temperature has reduced.

Get a long stick – the pole of a mop will do – and use it to close the lid of the pan. You can also try to turn it off using the pole. Never try to reach for the controls with your hands. You can also use the fire extinguisher if you cannot wait for the fire service to arrive. But for absolute safety, you should stand back or leave the building and wait for the fire service.

Maintaining the oil

Clean the oil regularly by filtering it properly at the end of each shift to remove small pieces of food or batter. You should also filter it during a shift. Fish, burgers and other frozen foods have a high rate of absorption because they have some water content, so fat spoilage is best controlled with a continual topping up with fresh fat or oil.

The breakdown of an oil will also depend upon its exposure to the oxygen in the air. The surface area of the oil is exposed to air, and the steam which is given off by the food during frying tends to create a blanket to protect the oil from oxygen. For this reason it is better to keep the oil busily frying food for as long as possible – oil held at frying temperature in an empty pan will deteriorate more quickly and begin to break down no matter how good its quality.

 Switching on only one pan in quieter periods means that you will not only save on gas usage but help maintain the oil.

When the oil has been used for some time it becomes old and if not topped up frequently or changed will give off an unpleasant smell. Old oil affects the quality and appearance of food. With filtration methods the oil can last longer and may not need to be changed as often.

CHANGING THE OIL

When I change the oil, one pan is shut down (I have a three-pan range) when the level of oil is low. The oil is transferred to the other pans and the empty pan is washed out. New oil is added into the pan. Some people do it a different way and just keep adding fresh fat into the pan.

When the fat is changed, it looks very clean and the chips appear quite white as it is difficult to brown them. Some customers think they do not look cooked – although they are – but when cooking in very clean oil it takes some time for food to get its golden brown appearance. If you want to avoid this don't change the oil but only add fresh.

Making to order

Making to order means creating food the instant the customer orders it, and to their specifications. From experience it is crucial to prepare foods well for customers who sit in the shop (if there are seating arrangements) as these customers will gladly tell you when something is wrong. For example, leaving chips in the chip box too long can make them dry, cold or even appear not fresh. This can also happen to food left for a certain amount of time in display cabinets.

This is a major mistake in fast-food outlets and it happens for a number of reasons:

☐ the customer is unable to wait for food to be made from fresh

☐ poor preparation

☐ carelessness as foods are not checked for quality

☐ uncertain levels of business

☐ chip-box and display cabinets are on at a low heat so the customer gets food that is cold.

To ensure that the customer always gets good quality food you must rely on your judgement. For example, if a portion of fish and chips is ordered and I feel that the chips in the chip-box are not up to standard I will prepare some new ones.

Alarm Bell

Food that has lost its quality because it has been on display for too long should not be sold.

Display cabinets should maintain the heat in food without causing dryness. Constant quality control is needed in the food preparation process – every food item sold should be rigorously monitored and only the best should be given to the customer.

Made-to-order food also means preparing foods to the customer's requirements, and it's best when food gets freshly prepared the instant the order has been taken. For instance, a customer may order chips made from fresh and not par-fried, or fish with very little batter. By fulfilling the customer's requirement you can ensure the products are made to order and that the food is freshly made and has not been left in the cabinet for 20 minutes.

PRACTISING

People who have never run their own fish and chip shop business may find there is a lot to learn. You may find that your working speed is slow, but with practice it will improve and later your movements will be quick and automatic. This is because we learn through repetition – it is the same for anything else you learn. It may take some time for you to get used to frying and serving. They must both be performed quickly to give customers a fast and efficient service. Only by practising, having a firm grasp of the basics, and then accelerating from there will you be competent in your role.

Multi-tasking

In the business world, multi-tasking is a well-known skill for managers and staff who have to be responsible for many tasks. Being a small business owner, you will probably have limited staff and be doing most, if not all, of the work. This means you will need to multi-task; for example, frying, heating up pies, and going for a bucket of chips are all done by you.

Multi-tasking also happens when you are preparing a lunch opening on your own, and staff arrive for a shift only when the shop is open. It also involves all other work behind the scenes.

As a small business owner you need to carry out most of the work and keep staff to a minimum. Multi-tasking includes:

❑ using two or three chip pans simultaneously;

❑ being able to deal with other tasks as well as keeping an eye on the fryer;

❑ supporting staff if necessary;

❑ being aware of sauce levels and ready to top up if required;

❑ observing the food in the display cabinet;

… and still being able to produce good quality food.

 If you have full-time staff it is a good idea to train them in multi-tasking so that they become more efficient workers; it also keeps the job interesting for people who warm to a challenge.

One particular member of our staff is very reliable and loyal and we have managed to train her well in multi-tasking. She works more hours than our other employees and has been with us the longest. That could be the reason why she is more competent in carrying out other tasks. Although she does not perform any frying duties, she is alert during shifts and she undertakes tasks as well as general serving and she performs well.

Sometimes multi-tasking is seen as ineffective because performing several tasks means that it takes longer to complete them and the quality is reduced. You will need to decide how much multi-tasking you will want to give employees. You may feel that having them perform several tasks during a service could affect the quality of their main role, which is to serve customers. I have found that it needn't be the case as long as you can delegate the tasks properly to staff and adjust them to the busyness of the opening.

Multi-tasking for you will include having to monitor stock levels and attending to the accounts side of the business. Being organised by giving a partner in the business and yourself separate responsibilities and tasks will lessen the work being done by one person.

Delegating tasks

To be an effective manager, and in this case a fast-food business owner, you need to delegate tasks to your employees. If you are not used to managing staff and telling them what to do, you may find it a little difficult at first.

Staff generally need guidance and you as their employer need to give them their roles and tasks. Staff should also be trained so they are able to handle the tasks you give them. You will probably find that when you delegate tasks, and therefore give the staff more responsibility, they will be more motivated.

Find a short time where staff aren't busy and ask them to do a job. It may be something like getting some fresh chips or a food product from the fridge. Whatever it is, it will save you a task.

Summary

We have looked in this chapter at how to cook different food types. There is a lot more to frying than people think and you need know-how and experience to get it right. We have also covered what to do to reduce risks and hazards when using frying equipment. There is a difference in the taste and texture of the food depending on the medium used and how well the oil is maintained so we have covered the processes required to get good results when foods are fried. In addition the chapter has covered using one and multiple chip pans and also multi-tasking and delegation.

8
EMPLOYING STAFF

In retail, people are employed to support a business. You might need part-time staff to come in on days when there is more trade. Or you might employ full-time staff who come in to work every day. What you decide will depend on the turnover and size of your premises. You may find that staff are not prepared to work as hard as you, but with decent rates of pay and a positive working environment good employees can be a valuable addition to the business.

Recruiting
Staff can be recruited fairly easily.

☐ People sometimes come into the premises and ask for work.

☐ Placing a notice in the shop window doesn't usually take long to generate some interest.

☐ You can list the vacancy with the local job centre and be placed on its online website. Using their service to find employees is free and you are able to list and manage your jobs all online.

☐ Put your details on a card at a local supermarket.

☐ You can place an advert in the local paper although there will be a cost.

☐ You could try speaking with owners of shops in the local area to let people know you are looking for staff.

Employing the right people
You can create an application form to show that it is a serious job; the form can include the requirement of references so you can determine each candidate's reliability. It's vital you employ the right type of person to help you.

Alarm Bell

Overlooking a proper selection process when recruiting may result in employing the wrong people, which will affect the performance of the business.

Spend time increasing the chances of selecting the right candidates – it will waste less time than taking on someone who may not be suited to this kind of employment. You want employees who are suited to the work, can perform well and are willing to work for a reasonable amount of time.

Here are some things to think about when recruiting:

☐ Does the person seem to be keen to learn and appear able to cope in a fast-food environment?

☐ Does the person have any experience in a catering outlet?

☐ Can you train them?

☐ Have they got a clear voice that can communicate well with customers?

☐ How long did they stay with their previous employer? This will help you find out if the person is reliable and will remain in the job for a reasonable length of time.

☐ Does the person have other commitments like another job or education?

☐ Is the person able to come in to work at short notice at unexpected times in the week when other staff are unable to work?

If you make a mistake in recruiting someone who may not be quite suited to the job it will be at your expense. I suggest you interview people before taking them on. Interviews allow you to sense what the person is like to work with and whether you think they will be a positive addition to your establishment.

Alarm Bell

Remember that it is not just the product which represents the business, it is the staff as well. Staff can add positive or negative energy to the workplace.

Past experience with previous workers means that whenever we recruit staff now we put our best efforts into trying to recruit a suitable candidate. We aim to find someone who will be committed to their role and can work in our establishment for some time – you don't want to be in a position where a worker you have trained to do the job leaves after a few months. When that happens not only do you have to start recruiting for someone again, you have to go through the training again too.

Part-time work is often suited to someone who is studying, or a young mum, for example. Some people do not want to work full time and need a part-time job which can fit around their life. If they find a job they like and which fits in with their other commitments they can be a loyal and hardworking member of staff.

Training

Training staff requires patience especially when they have no experience working in a fast-food environment. There is a lot to learn, like working systems and remembering menu prices. Even someone with experience takes time to get used to a pace and working methods that may differ from the environment of other outlets. Different members of staff learn at different speeds. Gradually they will improve and do their job well. Sometimes a part-time worker becomes full time once they are competent in their performance.

You will need to show them what to do, then observe them and correct them if needed. You can choose to take it easy with new staff or adopt a strict approach in training them to be ready more quickly for their post. At busy periods of the year – usually the winter when new staff join – they have to learn quickly as there is no time for slowly grasping the basics when there is a rush of customers in the premises.

Alarm Bell

There is a lot for new staff to learn and it takes time for them to get used to the role and work well.

Part-time workers must be trained and monitored constantly. If a worker comes in at weekends only and spends the rest of the week away from the premises, they can easily forget some parts of the job. Mistakes can be damaging to your profits. Price-calculation errors can happen, for example, and you can lose money. As some part-time staff spend most of the week attending other duties like going to college or looking after children, it is very understandable that they may forget some things. In these cases you need to observe them to spot any mistakes that may happen.

When training staff members:

☐ demonstrate a task and observe them doing it themselves

☐ highlight what they're doing well

☐ point out what they're doing wrong and make them aware of it

☐ be patient with trainee staff as it takes time for them to get used to the work

☐ delegate a variety of tasks so that they learn more, making them more efficient

☐ try to build a positive and friendly relationship with them to make them feel at ease, which can help their performance

☐ try to perform to a high level so that they can copy your approach.

Customer service

Organisations don't provide good service, it's the people who do. This is true for most businesses including the restaurant and fast-food sector. Companies that have a passion for high-quality customer service are more likely to keep the customer satisfied.

Alarm Bell

People will not judge you on just the product quality, but also on your customer service.

When your business, including customer service, is impeccable you will have satisfied customers. The business loses points if customer service standards are neglected.

Retail businesses are more vulnerable than others where the customer doesn't always have to go to the premises (such as insurance firms or online businesses for example), because the moment people walk through your door, anything negative is immediately apparent. First impressions really do count. In retail the premises, its management and its employees, represent everything and it is judged by service and product standards.

For example:

☐ If nobody smiles at the customer, it can affect their experience negatively.

☐ If a customer walks in and finds that you're talking on the phone they can be far from impressed.

☐ A lack of staff suggests that the business's management is bad.

☐ Not being served quickly enough shows incompetent service.

It is essential to be sincere with customers as it brings good feelings and trust. Customers need to be made to feel good spending money in your business. Your body language and tone of voice should come together well to create sincerity and appreciation for their business.

You and all members of staff should be friendly and helpful when serving customers. Serving should not be rushed. Give people time to put away their change and thank them before they leave the premises. There should be no hurry.

When you provide high levels of customer service, satisfied customers are likely to use your service again and are also happy to recommend you.

Communicating with customers

Research has shown that when customers have a strong relationship with the staff in a food establishment, they are very likely to go back often. (Of course this relationship must be backed by high-standard products.) In most small outlets at least two thirds of trade is from repeat customers. This fully emphasises the need for good relations with your customer.

In order to build rapport with customers, I like to find out their names, but it is crucial to remember them as it can be easy to forget. Repeat customers tend to order the same meals each time so you and staff should remember their preferences. This will show that you respect and care about the customer.

Alarm Bell

The member of staff who is serving is usually the first person that customers have contact with so it is important that they are friendly and smile when customers arrive.

It's a good idea to employ staff who don't shy away from conversation and enjoy communicating with people. Sometimes, staff just need some encouragement, so do make sure that staff who do not speak to customers are asked to do so as no one likes to be served by staff who seem miserable. You can start off a conversation with a customer and then try to work a member of staff into the discussion. Soon the employee will speak to the customer, or vice versa.

RAPPORT BUILDING

I find that when customers have been in a few times they will start off the conversation first as they know the service is friendly. It is interesting because you can learn a lot from customers. Most will have interesting professions and you can ask for advice on certain things.

A customer of mine works in an estate agency. She can advise me on the local property market and what to do in order to sell a house more quickly. Another customer I have works in a local supermarket. She regularly notifies me of any deals there are on soft drinks. Some customers come back from holiday and tell me what it was like and whether they recommend it. We have customers who bring us souvenirs each time they return from their holiday.

Building rapport is beneficial to both the business and the customer. It provides the customer with a better service and it can encourage repeat business.

From time to time there can be a problem with a lack of rapport with the customers, when staff don't put in enough effort to talk to customers. Some workers feel that they don't want people to talk to them when they go into a shop. However, experience tells me that most customers do want a bit of a chat and do not like boring service or talk that is too mechanical. Building good rapport with customers has a positive effect. A business can be transformed overnight by cheerful owners and friendly staff.

Some workers have the gift of the gab. Rapport building is easy for them and they really connect with customers. Our full-time member of staff does most of the talking to customers. Part-timers don't have to make too much effort as long as they talk back when a customer speaks to them. When customers get to know a member of staff well, conversation flows naturally and the atmosphere is good.

Staff who like to build rapport with customers will save you a lot of work. You can then turn more of your attention to creating good food.

MAKING PROMISES

A good salesperson can sell something to someone once. With the right approach and style of customer service you can sell your products to people again and again.

Don't make promises unless you are able to keep them. When we tell our customers that we can source the products they want or have an order ready at a particular time we make sure we do it. Reliability is very important and the key to any good relationship. You may need to think about what you're promising to your customers. If promises are not kept, it will let down the customer which will be annoying for them and may well lose you business.

Using the telephone

The telephone acts as a primary point of contact with customers, and the way you are on the phone will form the customer's first impression of your business.

ANSWERING THE PHONE

Answering the phone in the right way will benefit your establishment.

When answering the phone:

☐ Answer all calls within three rings.

☐ Sound warm and friendly. Your voice at the end of the telephone represents your business to the caller. Speak clearly with the right tone. The customer will be able to understand you more easily.

☐ Be courteous and welcome callers with the name of your establishment. For example, 'Hi…Tony's Fish bar… How may I help you?' Never use the speaker phone. Speaker phones make you sound very distant and give the impression that you are not concentrating on the call.

☐ If you need to put callers on hold, always ask them if it is all right to do so.

☐ Train everyone to answer the phone the same way. You could test this by calling yourself to see if they do so.

When the business is open, you won't always be able to answer the phone, but you should allow only trained staff to answer calls.

ANSWERING SERVICE

You should have call forwarding or an answering service. In opening hours you should really be sure someone will answer the phone when orders come through, even during busy periods. Customers will get annoyed when no one answers or if they hear a recorded voice asking them to leave a message.

You may want to have a professional message recorded for times when you are not available out of opening hours. You should also update the message, for instance if you are away on holiday. The message should say how long you will be away and when the business will re-open.

TAKING ORDERS BY TELEPHONE

You must be sure to take down the customer's order accurately. Try to give extra attention to taking orders on the phone, even though sometimes it can be difficult when there is a bad line or reception.

It is very annoying for the customer if they ring up with an order and come in half an hour later to collect it only to find that their order was taken down inaccurately. It is even worse if the customer doesn't check the order in the shop, assuming the staff have, and gets all the way home before finding the order incomplete.

To be completely sure of the accuracy of the order, read it back to the customer.

Listen to callers carefully. Ask for their name or give them a number so that the order can be identified when they come to collect it. The caller's telephone number should also be taken down in case an order is not collected. You can then chase up the customer to see what has happened. If you have a delivery service, don't forget to take down the customer's address.

Paying your staff

MINIMUM WAGE

Pay rates should be competitive and attractive, especially when employing staff for only a few hours in the evening. You need to be aware of the National Minimum Wage Act 1998 – there is a difference in the minimum hourly pay for workers depending on age. From October 2008 this was £5.73 per hour for workers aged 22 years and older, £4.77 per hour for workers aged 18-21, and £3.53 per hour for all workers under the age of 18 (who are no longer of compulsory school age). This changes annually so check your pay rates on www.hmrc.gov.uk/nmw and see if they are up to date.

What's important also is that the pay should be an amount that makes it worthwhile for your staff to leave their house for work. The type of scheme your employees are paid with can also affect their relationship with your business. Weekly pay seems to be more popular with staff.

Younger workers, depending on their age, can be restricted to certain hours and types of work. To find out more about this go to www.adviceguide.org.uk

EQUAL PAY

The Equal Pay Act 1970 protects men and women and ensures they receive the same amount of pay for the same job. When an amount of money is paid to someone doing a job, it must be exactly the same whether the person is male or female.

TAX AND NATIONAL INSURANCE

National Insurance contributions and tax must be paid. However, if part-time staff earn under the weekly allowance (for more information on how much you can earn before paying tax, see www.hmrc.gov.uk/rates/it), there are exemptions. It is essential to record the weekly wages in your accounts and have all part-time staff sign a P46 form. I advise you to consult your accountant for more information on this.

Health and safety at work

Staff have the right to work in a safe environment which protects their health and welfare. Food premises can be dangerous as people are working with equipment, gas-run fryers and using cleaning solutions.

EMPLOYER DUTIES

As an employer you will have responsibility for the welfare of your employees – that is to ensure that your workers are as safe as possible in the environment they're in. The kitchen is a high risk for hazards as there are hot items and sharp tools. You will need to give staff the proper training to handle tools and equipment within their role.

These are the general duties of an employer stated in the Health and Safety Act 1974:

☐ Making the workplace safe and without risks to health.

☐ Ensuring equipment is safe and that there are safe systems in place which are followed.

☐ Ensuring substances are moved, stored and used safely.

☐ Providing adequate welfare facilities.

☐ Ensuring employees are given adequate information, instruction, training and the supervision necessary to safely carry out their duties.

We never put any member of staff or customer in danger in our premises. As long as you are careful when working, and staff are aware of the hazards, there should not be any problems.

Alarm Bell

As the owner of the business it is your responsibility to ensure that the work of your employees is safe.

EMPLOYEE RESPONSIBILITIES

Workers must also take responsibility for their safety. They should also conform to the standards of the Health and Safety Act. This reduces the risks of accidents occurring since employer and employee are working together to eliminate potential hazards.

The Act states that workers should:

☐ Avoid wearing jewellery or unsuitable clothing that may affect their roles.

☐ Tie back or tuck away long hair to reduce the risk of it getting caught in equipment.

☐ Report any injuries, strains or illnesses suffered from their work.

☐ Tell their employer if something happens that might affect their ability to work – such as becoming pregnant or suffering an injury which may affect their work. They may need to be given time off until they're able to return to work.

☐ Let their employer know if they take any medication that makes them drowsy. This may be a risk when working with equipment.

☐ Take reasonable care when working so that they do not harm the welfare of fellow workers or members of the public.

☐ Co-operate with their employer in making sure they understand the risks of health and safety and have received proper training.

Keeping your staff motivated

It is important to motivate staff so their performance improves – this in turn benefits the business. People are, of course, motivated by money, but there are some other factors that can help motivate employees.

☐ People like to be made to feel important and of value to the place where they work.

☐ If you are enthusiastic it will rub off on employees and make the workplace a more enjoyable environment.

☐ When staff are relaxed they are better prepared for busy periods just before the adrenalin rush kicks in. Relaxed staff are happier, can increase productivity and be more positive. Customers will really notice the difference.

☐ Staff members must also be made aware of the seriousness of the work and that the standards of the business are high. You are investing your money in your employees so you want them to be able to perform well in every shift.

Staff usually want the following:

☐ Praise and recognition – either verbally, or financially (such as a bonus).

☐ Interesting work.

☐ To contribute to the decision-making.

☐ To be able to socialise with other staff.

☐ Good pleasant working conditions.

☐ Respect.

☐ Regular communication to be aware of what is going on.

PRAISING STAFF

If you want your staff to be motivated you need to reward them. When an employee has performed well it is nice to give them some positive comments – something as simple as 'Well done' or 'Thank you' can be a good motivator for them. When staff realise you recognise their efforts it builds their confidence. It is healthy to recognise their achievement.

 Staff who do well and give you good support could be given a pay rise or discounted meals.

I let my workers occasionally have a free meal when they finish their shift. It is good for relations and encourages them to be loyal in return.

INTERESTING WORK

Employees want their work to be interesting and even challenging. Many will enjoy busy openings as the work is not boring and time will go by quickly for them. Challenges can help motivate people. However, when challenges are too difficult people can lose motivation. Try to increase the work and tasks for workers so that they find their roles more dynamic.

 Remember that to motivate staff, you should also be motivated yourself.

DECISION-MAKING

Workers should be able to contribute to decision-making in the business. If employees are aware of what is going on in the business they can be more involved and it increases their attachment. The business can benefit from their opinions and ideas, and as a result there will be increased creativity in your business which will help increase its growth.

Advice from workers can be very helpful. As they are serving customers the most, they know what works and what doesn't. For example, we wanted to replace certain items on the menu, and we thought that using newer brands might be what our customers wanted. We got advice from our full-time member of staff who told us not to change as the regulars liked what we were selling already.

SOCIALISING WITH STAFF

A drink after work is the traditional way to bond, although there are alternatives such as bowling or other activities. If you are going to have a drink with your staff, it is wise not to get drunk. It will look very unprofessional in front of your employees.

Another problem with socialising with staff is that they may think they are your 'best pal' and not focus properly on their job. There needs to be both a friendly atmosphere and a serious work ethic. Employees should get the message to work hard and play hard.

GOOD PLEASANT WORKING CONDITIONS

Staff want to work in clean tidy areas so it is important to keep the premises clean for employees as well as for customers. Being a food premises, more cleaning is needed to reduce smells and to keep the premises tidy. Our policy is to be sure the premises is fit to work in most of the time.

RESPECTING STAFF NEEDS

Sometimes staff members may have to take time off unexpectedly. As long as the requests are not frequent, granting them graciously can in return cause staff to work harder to make up for lost effort. I try to adapt to their needs especially when they need to be away from work for good reason.

 Your efforts in keeping staff happy will create workers who are more productive.

Treating good employees well will encourage their loyalty to you. When attention is paid to the needs of staff, it creates more unity and they bring more positive energy to the workplace.

COMMUNICATING WITH STAFF

Staff need clear goals at work. The mind works better when it knows what its target is. Staff should be reminded of the objectives of the business and how their roles can meet them. Employees are more productive when they are clear about their purpose.

Sometimes there is little time to have a staff meeting or discussion, which can make it hard to communicate with staff. I find it very effective to write notes, which can be reminders or objectives, on a piece of paper. The staff notice it when the premises is quiet and are happy to read it. They are then clear and aware of the goals.

I use a mixture of written information and verbal delegation, which seems to work. Written information backs up the verbal communication which can often be forgotten.

You will probably communicate a lot with your main members of staff, such as full-time workers. Those who have been working for a reasonable length of time will probably understand the business well. They will understand your needs as the business owner and will be able to take in any issues or plans that you have.

Employee problems

Employees play a key part in the operation of the business and their issues will affect the business. The main issues are their performance during a shift and their reliability in coming into work. Some of our part-time staff have young children and sometimes are not able to work because their child is sick or they have other childcare problems. As a parent they have every right to attend to the needs of their child.

Punctuality can be also an issue. I used to have an employee who was always at least 15 minutes late. In that time, several customers had already entered and left the premises. Being this late is disrespectful to the job and to the employer. Most staff do not have a serious problem with timekeeping, but if it happens the worker should be spoken to and a warning given if they are frequently late.

Common problems with employees in this business are:

☐ frequently not able to come into work

☐ frequently late for work

☐ don't make an effort to talk to customers

☐ poor performance at work

☐ lack of rapport with the customers

☐ struggle to get the hang of the speed needed in the work

☐ don't try to improve their performance.

Performance issues

The performance of staff will affect the business greatly. For example:

☐ Staff may not take the job as seriously as you and their incompetence will affect your business.

☐ They may not follow requests well. Staff like this need to be made sure they realise that they are working in a service and that the way they work will hurt the business.

☐ Workers who are not disciplined think it is easy to get way with things. As it is your business that is getting hit hard, you should make it clear that they must raise their performance level or you will be better off with a replacement.

Have a one-to-one talk with your workers with performance problems. You need to assess the situation. They may in fact be trying, but it might be taking them a little more time to get the hang of things. If you support them properly, they will soon be able to grasp the working methods and better support your establishment.

 Some workers just need a bit of encouragement to perform better and to learn new skills.

MONITOR YOUR STAFF'S PERFORMANCE

Staff should always be improving their performance – just as you are. They should not stay at the same level. Once a member of staff learns how to do the job they often do not want to learn any more. Many do not want to do any more work than they did on the previous shift, but it is important to delegate some more tasks to employees.

Don't be afraid to give staff a little more work than they are used to. We are creatures of habit, and if you avoid delegation at the start it will become a routine in which your failure to manage staff properly will affect their efficiency and contribution to the shop.

The quality of work should be monitored as staff can reduce their standards, by working more slowly or making frequent mistakes. Ideally, staff should get better at their job at every shift.

Try to give more attention to new staff. They will need support before their performance can equal the staff who have been working longer in your establishment. You will be able to tell which employee best supports your business – they will generally lead newer members of staff. From this staff member you can get feedback on other staff's performance.

COMMON MISTAKES

It is not unusual to miss items off a customer's order. It is embarrassing when a customer realises they are missing a bag of chips or a cup of gravy. If they come back you should always apologise; some may not come back to get their item and you normally won't see them again.

This mistake happens because of inadequately-trained staff or poor working systems. Most small food takeaway outlets do not have sophisticated computer systems to input orders. All large fast-food chains have a system in place to record orders; the price and the change required is all worked out by their systems. It is important to have at least a pen and paper system.

During a busy opening it can be possible that staff will forget to take money from the customer. Sometimes even the customer forgets to pay. It is always a good idea for the customer to pay for their food as soon as their order has been taken down.

Alarm Bell

Always serve the customers in the order they are in the queue. Serving the wrong customer first when others have been waiting longer is not good practice.

Working systems

A system of working should be followed during every shift so that it becomes a habit and that staff will do it automatically.

Every order should be clearly written down on paper so that the writer, and others, can read it. Staff should be trained to ask the customer whether they want salt and vinegar on their food. If they do, the letters 'SV' can be put on the order to indicate this. If not you can write 'no SV' on the order. If the customer wants only salt on the order we write 'JS'; if only vinegar we write 'JV'.

We usually ask the customer to pay first, and a 'P' is written to indicate that the order has been paid for. This system minimises mistakes and ensures that the customer's order is prepared correctly. I make sure that each member of staff can fully understand the system and then whenever an order is taken over by another staff member it can be followed without complications.

At the end of an order, the items on the list should be ticked off one by one to be sure that the order is complete. This is especially important when working on large orders. It is too easy to miss off smaller items like a bread roll or a sausage.

Alarm Bell

Make sure your systems are not too complicated as it will take longer for workers to adapt to them.

During a shift be sure that:

- ☐ you have at least two working calculators

- ☐ you have pens and paper

- ☐ staff follow the working system

- ☐ new workers are trained to use the system.

You can of course design a working system tailored for your own business. Try it out for a few weeks to test its efficiency. If it needs tweaking change it so that it better supports you.

Setting up a routine

It is important to set up a routine and ideally a timetable. You could carry a small notebook with you so that at quiet times of the day you can look up what you should be ordering. It is easy to forget something in a small catering outlet as there is a limited amount of staff and the main person (usually the owner) will be doing most of the work both at opening times and behind the scenes.

A routine needs to be in place in the daily running of the operation. In a husband/wife or partnership business, each individual can be responsible for certain tasks.

It is advisable that each person takes turns and sometimes swaps roles so that when one person is unavailable, the work can still get done and be handled properly by another.

For example in a husband/wife business, it helps if both can work in the position as 'fryer' and both have equals skills in serving. When one person can manage multiple roles in the operation, it enables the business to continue running with the support of staff when a key person is unavailable for work.

In a partnership with a husband/wife or partner it is not uncommon for the couple to remind each other of what needs to be ordered or done. Although this is effective, it means that you are relying on the other person to prompt you, and this in turn increases the chances of a mistake happening.

It can help if different people have different roles. For example, one person can handle the paperwork – the admin side of the business. Another person can be responsible for ordering supplies. Take a look at the two roles and their responsibilities below.

Stock manager	Office manager
Order potatoes	Pay utility bills
Order fish	Pay supplier bills
Order burgers	Pay business rates
Order fried chicken	Pay loan payments or rent
Order sausages	Pay employees
Order other food items	Do the book-keeping
Order non-food items	Pay waste collection services
Monitor all stock	Keep and file records of paperwork

You can see that neither role is easy, and both require organisation and discipline. If at all possible it's best to have someone for each role, although there are people who have managed shops on their own with the support of staff.

Reducing the risks

It's important to minimise the risk of accidents happening. Staff need to be trained properly when using equipment and to be made aware of any dangers. When using cleaning substances, you must provide staff with protective clothing as the chemicals in solutions can be harmful.

Being in a food business means that the premises must be kept clean and floors mopped regularly. After cleaning, surfaces will be wet for a short time. To avoid people slipping on the floor, clean the floors when there are fewer people on the premises. Staff could slip and hurt themselves, and if their accident was bad, they could sue for negligence. The same goes for customers or people not related to the business. Remember that children and elderly people are at greater risk.

FRYING RANGES

A range is a potential for danger because of its heat and high temperatures – but risks can be reduced to a minimum with careful operation. Workers should be fully trained to use the fryer and employees who have not had any training must not be allowed to operate it. To reduce risks further workers need to co-operate and be careful working near range areas.

Staff who have not had sufficient training should never attempt to use the fryer.

When you are using large frying ranges there are large amounts of oil heated to high temperatures. It's important to take precautions so that you don't get hurt. Here are some important things to remember:

☐ Place chips and other food items carefully in the pan to reduce oil splashing.

☐ Oil temperatures need to be controlled carefully to reduce the chances of overheating which may ignite flames.

☐ Oil that is overheated should be cooled – turn down the thermostat and top up with fresh fat.

☐ Be sure to train staff properly in using frying equipment and to know what to do when a fire occurs.

The frying range is possibly the most likely part of the premises for a serious accident to occur. The oil is heated to high levels, and because it is always in the vicinity of the working area, it needs to be your main focus in preventing hazards.

OTHER WORKING EQUIPMENT

A potato chipper has sharp blades, so whoever takes it apart for cleaning must handle it carefully and be aware of its dangers. Staff should also be told not to put their hand inside the chipper. It can be tempting to do when the chipper is too full of potatoes, or one is stuck causing it to stop working. It is best to take the hood off and take out some potatoes. Be sure to train staff properly to do it, or tell them that when this happens they must let you know and not tackle it themselves.

Kebab-cutting blades can be dangerous. Staff must be trained properly before they are allowed to handle them. Train and observe them before leaving workers to use the blade without your supervision.

FIRE-FIGHTING EQUIPMENT

The premises must have adequate fire-fighting equipment such as fire extinguishers and a fire blanket. Fire extinguishers should be serviced each year by a certified fire-safety inspector. We have never used any of the fire extinguishers or the fire blanket and hope we never have to. But they have to be there ready for use. You should teach staff how to use them just in case you are out of the premises.

OIL FUMES

Being a fish and chip business means that there will be fumes from frying. The fryer is on constantly even when nothing is being fried. Your premises needs to be well ventilated to allow oil fumes to escape or it will be unpleasant to breathe. Ventilate areas by opening windows and doors to let air flow as congested oil fumes are not safe for employees or customers.

POTENTIAL HAZARDS

You have a duty to spot all potential hazards in the premises. It is also advisable to have equipment checked from time to time. You should do the following:

☐ Have a gas engineer to check gas lines.

☐ Check electrical wires, sockets and plugs for wear and tear.

☐ Be sure that fire exits are easily accessible.

☐ Be sure the first aid is available when it is needed.

☐ Know what to do in an emergency.

Summary

We have seen how the performance of staff will be affected by your ability to manage them. Of course the standard of each employee's work is different, but when there is an issue with employees it is your responsibility to train and communicate with them. Most importantly, along with staff being able to work to a high standard, they must be able to build rapport with the customers. As well as managing staff, setting up a routine can help a premises run smoothly and much more efficiently. We have also looked at keeping the premises and the staff safe.

9
ADVERTISING FOR MORE BUSINESS

Advertising a product or service creates awareness and needs to be done to attract more business and to increase sales. It pays to do a little advertising before you actually begin trading – it lets people know that your business exists; if necessary it tells them that it has been taken over and is under new management. Advertising costs money but must be done in any business for it to increase its turnover.

In practical terms advertising is a way to let people know you are there. If you are offering a delivery service, for example, you can place an advert in the local newspaper, or you can print leaflets to be delivered door to door. You could also have a website, use the radio or place an advert in a trade magazine.

 Advertising seems to work best when several methods are used, not simply one technique.

The main purpose of advertising is to:

☐ Let people know about your service and that you are open for business.

☐ Create desire for your product

☐ Inform customers of your unique selling point (for example, having more product variety and an interesting menu can make your establishment stand out from the competition).

☐ Promote products and special offers.

☐ Give a professional image and promote the business by having a menu for customers to take away.

Advertising can help your business in different ways. For example, it can help you find new customers who order a large amount of food. I have a couple of customers who work at a business retail park and they order for a lot of staff in their offices. I initially dropped off some menus which caught their attention, and now they are regular customers.

Apart from increasing sales, advertising also builds your brand.

A good method to decide how to advertise is to try a few things within your budget and see what works best. Then you can concentrate on those.

Newspaper advertising

Adverts in local papers get a lot of exposure and help make people aware of the business. There is a variety of ways to advertise in newspapers:

☐ **Classified advertising**: this contains only words and is usually the cheapest option.

☐ **Display and semi-display**: this type of advert is bigger and has more detail. It often appears in editorial pages and can contain pictures.

☐ **Menus and leaflets**: these can be inserted in newspapers, for which you pay a fee.

☐ **Advertising feature:** which features you and the business; suppliers can also be featured if they contribute to the fee.

You need to give some thought to the design and text. Research shows that adverts on right-hand pages catch the readers' attention most often. It is helpful to include a product promotion or special offer which will catch people's attention – for example, a meal offer to buy one fish and chips and get one free. The promotion can be valid for a certain amount of time such as a few weeks to a month (make sure to include that in the advert).

It's a good idea to work closely with the person who places your adverts for you – the advert gives a message about your service and brand and they will be able to give you advice about that.

An advert in a paper must stand out – the readers can easily overlook it as they scan the pages.

NEGOTIATING PRICES

It's always worth negotiating prices for advertising in publications. The key to advertising is repetition so it is advisable to place several adverts throughout the year – the advantage is that you should be able to get a discount for booking multiple advertisements. Media sales are often flexible as they want to earn commission and will work to get your business.

Listing your business in directories

Advertising your business in the *Yellow Pages* and phone directories can also help – but remember you will be in competition with other food businesses, so think carefully about how to make your advert stand out.

Menus and leaflets

A leaflet can list all your products and prices, and give potential customers information on your service. Leaflets are reasonably cheap to produce and a powerful form of direct marketing; as such they can be a very effective part of advertising for a small food premises. You can use them to promote your service in the local area by dropping them through letterboxes. It helps if you combine leaflet distribution with a newspaper advertisement (preferably a paper which gets circulated for free).

PRODUCING MENU AND LEAFLETS

Menus and leaflets can be created with the use of a computer software program and a colour printer. Nowadays, with modern software packages, near-professional leaflets can be created at home. If, however, you want to save time doing this, or you don't have the equipment you need, you can use leaflet printing services for a fee. They will create very attractive and professional-looking leaflets that are eye-catching and are reasonably affordable.

Leaflets can come in sizes A4, A5, A6 or 1/3 A4 and can be single or double sided. When using a service, you should be clear about your requirements. The lettering on the menu should be attractive with the prices clearly visible. Some companies will let you supply your own artwork to place on the leaflet. You can also have photographs of your products included on the menu.

Alarm Bell

When producing your own leaflets be sure to check the content thoroughly – for spelling and information – before printing.

ESSENTIALS TO HAVE ON THE LEAFLET

☐ the name of the premises with contact telephone number and address

☐ the opening times

☐ well-designed logos and, ideally, pictures of the food

☐ a list of all products sold, including prices

☐ special offers, such as money-off vouchers.

It is a good idea to include something that tells people that your service is different from your competitors. It could be that the fish used is the freshest fish available or that all the pizzas are made from fresh. It could be a free delivery service or very good value for money meal deals. Or perhaps an order over a certain amount receives a large bottle of soft drink.

PRINTING THE LEAFLETS

It's best not to print too many leaflets at a time because if you increase prices or add some new products, the menu will be out of date. I print enough to last up to five months in the year. Every time I have new leaflets printed, new special offers are added and placed on the front of the leaflet where they can be clearly seen.

DISTRIBUTING THE LEAFLETS

Once you have your menus, they should be distributed to people's homes. This is direct marketing. There are services that will distribute your menus in a chosen area or district for a fee. I prefer to save on such costs and deliver the leaflets myself, although using a service will save you time.

You can also:

☐ leave some leaflets on the shop counter for customers to take away;

☐ put a menu in the carrier bag when you are serving customers;

☐ visit shops in your local area and ask to leave them some leaflets;

☐ drop some leaflets off at a business park if there is one nearby with office units. You may gain some new customers – working people might want to try something different from their usual lunch. I drop off leaflets at least once every six weeks – although offices usually keep hold of a menu at their reception desk, sometimes people lose them.

Timing your advertising

Be sure to budget well for your advertising campaign as the key to advertising is repetition. Research clearly shows that it takes time for an advert to take effect. First-time adverts can go practically unnoticed and are forgotten very quickly. When people have seen an advert a few times they start to notice it, think about it, and later decide to buy. Remember to keep your advertising consistent so that it will capture people's attention.

 It is ideal to do some regular promotion every month. This will ensure new customers are found and that people know that the business exists.

Try to choose the best times to carry out marketing campaigns. A slow start in the new year, for example, requires a much-needed boost from advertising. It's good to distribute leaflets on a Thursday – next to pay day (Friday), and near the weekend. It can also be effective to distribute them on a Sunday or early in the week when people may not be that busy – this will give them enough time to have a think and decide to use your service later in the week.

Increasing your customer base

The purpose of advertising is to attract new customers to use the service and then give them a good long-lasting impression so that they will use the service again. Once a customer has come in because of advertising, whether they come back will depend on the food and service. The aim is to have, as far as possible, a continuous amount of people visiting the premises.

Starting with **advertising**, you attract customers and create awareness that your business exists. Then it's vital that the **service** is good – when a new customer orders you must deliver quality food and service to create higher chances of a repeat sale. **Regular advertising** maintains awareness of the business and creates new customers, who need to receive good service – and so on.

To continue to have new people trying your service it's important to advertise regularly. New housing developments may have been completed, for example, and people who have just moved in may not know that there is a food business nearby. By making these potential customers aware of your premises they could soon become part of your customer base.

The power of word-of-mouth

Be it good or bad, word-of-mouth has the power to affect people in a far deeper way than any other form of marketing. Negative word-of-mouth in catering can cause consequences which are hard to correct.

 Never underestimate what word-of-mouth can do to your business.

Research shows that dissatisfied customers will tell five to ten people about their experience. Those people will inform around the same number of people and so on. It works the same way when there is positive word-of-mouth about your business – people will take a liking to your business even if they haven't tasted your food.

Satisfied customers will tell their family and friends about your service. There are successful shops that do very little advertising to enhance their business but continue to do well through promotion from satisfied customers. Keeping customers happy with the service will mean that they promote the shop in a positive way to their friends, colleagues and family.

 Word-of-mouth is the best form of marketing for business and the most cost effective.

Perhaps the premises has undergone a full refurbishment or the menu has become much more exciting. Things like this will encourage people to talk in a positive way about the business.

WHY WORD-OF-MOUTH WORKS

The reason word-of-mouth is proven to work is that it does not come from the business itself, or from a paid actor on television. The people who are talking about the business don't have anything to gain. If a friend recommends a film that is good, you are far more likely to watch it than if you have just seen the trailer or a promotion in a magazine.

 Research shows that people trust the opinions of other consumers. If they hear that someone who has used a product says it is good they are more likely to buy that product.

I had an experience where I was looking for a new internet provider, and in the end I chose the provider that a friend had recommended to me. My friend told me that even though the company was smaller and less well known than other larger ones, it was rare for a disconnection with the server to happen. I went with the company that was recommended to me and find the service to be very good (and I very rarely get disconnected).

NEGATIVE WORD-OF-MOUTH

The disadvantage is that a product or service can get negative word-of-mouth – this should be avoided at all costs. If you're not careful it can destroy the business. Think about times when you have had a bad experience with a particular service or product – I am sure you did not speak about them kindly. Word-of-mouth in this business is influenced by your product and customers' satisfaction. Your service must be of a high standard so that there is nothing bad to say.

Having your own website

A website is inexpensive to set up – if you have reasonable computer skills, you can attempt to build a website yourself. You can use a software package to help you, or a website-building service.

A website can showcase your business and you can add photos of your premises with some history about yourself in the business. It should have a listing of your products and any unique selling points. It is also a chance to promote the benefits of eating fish and chips and expose the myth of fast food being unhealthy. You can also educate customers about how much work is done to make good fish and chips and other products, which will let customers know the value of what you're selling.

If you are confident about the service you provide, you could have a section for customers to leave comments. Positive feedback will benefit the business as it will boost the reputation of it being a good place to visit in the area.

Online ordering

Internet shopping has become the norm, and there is a trend beginning in online takeaway ordering. There are services online that allow your business to be added to their database for a fee. You receive a webpage for your business which displays your food products and menu. It acts like a search directory for registered takeaways. When people are searching on the site, it lists the registered fast food businesses within their area.

When someone places an order it usually gets sent to you in a number of ways – by phone, mobile text message, fax or email. The internet is forever expanding and its usage increasing – ordering takeaway food online could soon be as common as it is now to pick up the phone to call for a pizza delivery.

There are many advantages to ordering takeaway food online.

☐ During busy periods, people often struggle to get through on the phone.

☐ Phone orders not only involve someone being available, but are prone to mistakes such as missing off an item on a customer's order or forgetting to ask them for their phone number or address.

☐ The online system totals up the order which is more efficient than doing it manually.

☐ Purchasing online is easy and convenient and your webpage will get bookmarked by people who have used the service

☐ Your webpage address can be printed onto leaflets and included in newspaper advertising and other promotional items to encourage people to use it.

Listing your business with these sites is ideal if you provide a delivery service. The disadvantage is that you will be competing for business online with other takeaway businesses in your area. However, using this method will surely gain you more business.

Radio

Radio reaches lots of people. It is a good idea to use a local radio station that targets people in your region. People listen to the radio in the car, at home and at work and may hear your advert. Mention in the commercial any special offers you have so that when people hear it, it catches their attention.

Keep in mind that a radio commercial is short and has only a short time to interest people. It needs to be interesting and catchy for it to be able to spark interest. Before you make an advert, listen to your local station for a while to get a feel for what sounds good and what seems to be effective.

Free publicity

Local newspapers may give your business coverage because of a situation or an event that is likely to draw some interest. Perhaps you have just re-opened a shop that was closed for some time and have made some improvements to the premises, or maybe you have fully renovated the shop and made the brave decision to serve new foods that will make the business unique. Whatever it is, it has to attract people for the newspaper to be interested. If an editor thinks it is worthy of a press release, you should get that coverage without charge.

Once your business is in the local paper it will be noticed both by people who have used your service and those who haven't. It will generate positive interest and will not have cost you anything.

PROMOTION

Regular meal offers that are likely to encourage repeat business work well. You will always get interest when meals are very good value for money. I have a burger meal special on the menu for just £2.20. Customers try it and tend to return and buy it again. This works because people feel it saves them money and it encourages them to try new products. Such competitive price promotions make people more aware of certain products and send the message of good value which can keep customers loyal.

It works well to have regular promotions when certain products are not selling as well as others. By promoting them you can increase their sales and as a result they become more popular.

 If a new item has been added to your product-base you can launch it by putting it in a meal deal – that way people become aware that it is on your menu.

When you want to promote certain products, let your customers know. They need to be told about your products – perhaps there is something they may not have tried but would give a go if they knew more about it, and saw that there was a promotion.

Apart from including those products on leaflets and by talking to your customers, the products can be explained on your shop menu. Make sure there are pictures of the products displayed so that potential customers can see exactly what the products are.

 Use the shop window to create a display of special offers to catch the attention of passing trade.

SHOP SIGNAGE

The signage for your premises gives your business its identity and catches the attention of passing trade. Effective shop fronts that show their products and service – which have the signs designed to display the main products you sell – attract the right customers.

There are custom-designed shop signs available which can be brightly lit up at night, which are a good form of constant advertising. People should be able to see from a distance and it can be an ongoing advertisement for passing trade. Ineffective signage that is unclear won't attract potential customers into your business.

CARRIER BAGS

Carrier bags can be printed with your shop name, so your customers and other people see it. People often re-use carrier bags so they will see the name again and remember it. Having bags printed will cost more than usual bags but it can be a useful tool in your advertising campaign.

T-SHIRTS

T-shirts can be printed both front and back with the business name and worn by you and members of staff. Whenever you're out of the premises, your business can be seen by people and more awareness will be created.

CAR

The same can be done using your car. Your business name and phone number can be displayed on the doors of the car. This is great for an outlet that provides a delivery service. It promotes your business and advertises your service whenever you are driving.

Summary

We have looked at many advertising methods to help you publicise the business. Newspaper advertising and posting leaflets and menus work the best, along with positive referral from cutomers. Using the radio can be an effective part of the advertising campaign making the business much more known. With technology advancing quickly and internet usage being common, it could be useful to have a website. Having your trading name printed on bags can also help in business promotion although it can be costly. However, wearing a T-shirt which carries the name of the premises looks professional and is paid for only once. The business needs some regular advertising each year to maintain its profile. Without advertising, new businesses that open will be happy to take your customers away with their own promotional campaigns.

10
RUNNING THE PREMISES

Energy management

All businesses benefit from good energy management since it reduces costs and increases profit. Using gas and electricity is a forever expense so it makes sense to choose a supplier that can offer competitive prices. There will be a lot of both gas and electricity used in most catering establishments. The frying range will run on gas and electricity, and the cooker is used daily. Other equipment will operate with electricity.

CONTROLLING YOUR ENERGY BILLS

The amount of energy you use will depend on the opening hours – a premises that opens for over ten hours a day will of course have a higher bill than one that opens for only five hours a day. The cost of keeping fluorescent lighting inside the premises and shop signs brightly lit will be expensive for long periods. Both gas and electricity must be managed effectively to reduce emissions and costs. Some suppliers can fix your utility prices for a number of years which will help you avoid any unwanted price increases.

WATER USAGE

You will need to use water daily, but not as often as gas and electricity. In chapter two I talked about the advantage of not having a water meter as premises that have a water meter installed will measure exactly how much is used and be charged accordingly. Water must be controlled and managed so that it is not used to excess and its cost minimised.

OTHER METHODS TO REDUCE ENERGY COSTS

It is a good practice to switch off unnecessary lights especially after closing time. Leaving any lights on will make costs mount up. The same goes for equipment in the premises. If there is accommodation above the premises make sure that when no one is there the lights are turned off, as well as televisions and other electrical equipment. Gas usage in the accommodation area can be reduced by turning down the thermostat – the cost of heating rises eight per cent for every 1°C increase.

I recommend checking your consumption of energy regularly and comparing costs against the year before. There are many energy suppliers that can save quite a substantial amount of money from your current bill.

Protecting the premises

The shop premises needs to be secure both when the business is in operation and when it has closed. When open it needs to be safe from theft and scams, and when closed from burglary and damage.

A premises should not make itself vulnerable to crime. Depending on the type of area where the premises is situated, it could well be a target for youths or adults. The people who cause damage have no idea, nor do they care, about the amount of effort and investment put into a business.

SHUTTERS

The premises should have sufficient security to protect contents such as valuable working equipment. If there is a break-in, equipment may be stolen or, even worse, the premises could get vandalised or be at risk of fire damage. Most catering shops have steel shutters which prevent any unwanted break-ins.

Alarm Bell

Shops without shutters have to pay higher insurance premiums.

I have a friend who runs his own catering outlet that did not have steel shutters. His shop is very near to a pub, and he gets a decent amount of business from people coming out of the pub. Unfortunately he has had lots of trouble from people causing damage to his window; it was broken twice in six months. He said that even though he has insurance it was pointless to claim from it as his premiums would go up – so he decided to replace the glass himself. He has now installed shutters to protect his premises. This is especially important when a premises is in a high risk location or area. Small quiet community areas can be very vulnerable to vandalism.

WORKING WITH THE AUTHORITIES

Reducing youth crime is a part of the government's effort to build safer communities and tackle social exclusion. Reforms have been put in place which aim to prevent offending by children and young people. You may want to work closely with the local police to tackle crime within the area.

Police community support officers assist the police force in reducing crime in community areas. When these areas are in need of help, they will request police assistance. These officers do not have the same powers as regular police but can be a very helpful addition to putting a stop to anti-social behaviour.

They also communicate with troublesome youths and people who are a danger or a nuisance to the neighbourhood. There are usually discussion groups held at local community centres that involve local people contributing ideas to solve problems. Community support officers will also be present at these gatherings to listen to people's input.

AN ALARM SYSTEM

Every shop premises should have a security system to sound an alarm when an intruder is in the premises. Not only is there valuable working equipment but the shop itself must be protected. Shutters will keep people from getting in but there are other ways to break in, such as behind the premises. Unless there are bars fitted or a steel door, it is still possible for intruders to enter. Without an alarm system, the premises can get vandalised and even be set on fire. If the premises does not have an alarm, it is very important to install one as soon as possible.

Alarm Bell

Having an alarm is crucial for safety and protection from theft, vandalism or fire damage.

Restoring a premises after a fire costs a lot of money. Having an alarm in place will protect the premises and its equipment. If you are living above the premises, it will also provide security and protect your belongings when you're away from the property.

The alarm should be turned on every time there is no one in the premises. Memorise the security code and only give it to somebody in a position of responsibility such as the manager. You may want to use numbers you can easily remember – I use my daughter's birthday. For more security you could change the code every few months to minimise risks.

In most alarm systems certain areas of the building can be exempt from intruder alert. This means that suppliers can have a key to access the premises for deliveries but will not set off the alarm.

Protecting yourself

Caution is important in business as you have everything at stake – both the business premises and the contents inside the building. Some burglaries are actually 'inside jobs' where the burglar is, or was, an employee who observed what was valuable and worked out a way to enter the premises.

My advice is to be friendly to people and staff but try to withhold some private information about yourself like your exact home address (if you do not live above the premises) and other personal information. Remember they are your staff and employees and, although healthy relationships help both parties, they are not meant to be close personal friends.

INSTALLING A CAMERA

A camera can be used to monitor customers and staff and to assess the operation during service. The image can be transferred to a television and then be recorded on tape with sound. You can also protect yourself from theft by placing a clearly visible camera.

The main benefits of having a camera are that it:

☐ records scams and thefts

☐ puts off staff who could be dishonest and skim the cash register

☐ monitors the opening to see what can be improved in service

☐ allows you to observe staff performance

☐ gives you peace of mind.

Prevention is better than cure – some people will try out scams in which they claim that they have paid for something or that they are owed change. You can play the tape back to see what actually happened. It's very useful as your attention is on so many things in service it makes it very difficult to see everything that is going on and the camera can see things that you can't. I have witnessed very few scams and theft in the business but it can happen.

Recordings can also be useful in assessing how you operate when the business is open. You may not realise how you move and operate when working and it lets you see the operation from a different perspective.

You are vulnerable to criminal activity when you're running a retail business and it is very important to minimise chances of a theft. Cameras make the area safer to work in for you and your employees.

MONITORING STAFF

Cameras can also be used to monitor staff performance, including your own, during an opening. You can see what mistakes happened and what needs to be improved. A camera can be aimed at the cash register to monitor that cash is handled correctly in service and that no one is skimming the till.

TYPES OF CAMERA

There are many camera set-ups available on the market. What type you have is up to you – as long as there is one in the premises it should be sufficient to warn people and make the premises a safer place to work in. Although retailers with larger premises may need more sophisticated cameras like CCTV with split screen display and zoom, these are not really necessary for small food businesses. They are more suited to retailers such as newsagents which usually have goods displayed that are within the reach of shoplifters.

Disposing of waste

There is a lot of food waste and rubbish to dispose of in a food business.

There are waste collection services that charge a weekly fee to rent a bin. They are fairly reasonably priced and the waste is collected every week. The size of the bin will depend on how much waste there is and the size of the catering establishment. My premises has tables for customers to eat in, and there is more food waste as a result.

Alarm Bell

Do not be tempted to put food waste in a residential bin – if caught you will be issued with a fine.

You must use a waste collection service and the council will sometimes come and check that the waste is being disposed of properly. They will need to see the paperwork relating to the waste collector.

RE-USING FAT

Old fat from catering outlets and restaurants can also be used as car fuel to be run in diesel engines. This is called bio-diesel, a substitute fuel from renewable sources that does not add new carbon to the atmosphere. The fat must be properly filtered and tax is paid on how much is used. There are collection services that pick up used fat from restaurants and food outlets – they don't usually pay for it, but the waste is picked up without charge.

Maintaining equipment

Without working equipment the premises cannot operate. Equipment must be well maintained to stay in good working order. Replace any faulty cooking equipment or utensils as soon as you need to. You don't want the equipment to fail just when you need it most. As mentioned previously, try to get the previous owners of the business to leave contact numbers of tradespeople to maintain and fix equipment. If not, a gas engineer is best suited to remedy range problems and can also tackle issues with other equipment.

 TOP TIP Putting effort into maintaining working equipment will extend its life and it will serve you longer.

You should train staff to take care when using working equipment and show them that they have a responsibility to maintain its condition.

THE FRYING RANGE

The frying range must be serviced every year to keep it in good working order and to ensure its safety. It is the most expensive piece of equipment in a fish and chip shop and must be looked after to reduce the chance of a breakdown.

It is quite unlikely that the frying range will fail to work altogether. It is more likely that one pan may refuse to turn on, while the others are still working. Sometimes a problem is small and if you are technically-minded you can attempt to fix the issue yourself before calling a professional. It might be as simple as some dirt in the pilot which needs to be cleared.

 Alarm Bell When dealing with bigger range problems be on the safe side and leave it to a qualified engineer.

The range must also be cleaned regularly. Remove the glass by sliding the pieces out of their slots and washing them in the sink. Oil filter trays can also be removed. The oil that has passed through these trays onto the range must be washed out using a good cleaning liquid. As the grease will stick, it is best to spray on a kitchen grease remover first and leave it on for around 20 minutes prior to scrubbing.

The chip-box must also be washed out. It has a filter through which excess fat runs onto a tray; the fat from this tray can be emptied back into the pan. The exterior of the range needs to be cleaned as well as the interior, especially the top, the sides and the bottom.

 The range should be cleaned just after an opening when it is still hot. This makes it easier to get rid of grease and grime.

PEELERS AND CHIPPERS

Potato peelers and chippers should also be serviced annually as they can have unexpected problems. The cutting blades from potato chipping machines should be checked from time to time – you will have a chance to do it when the machine is taken apart to be cleaned. The worst thing that can happen is that fragments of metal may come off the blade and can be dangerous. Be sure to check the appearance of each blade and that they are all intact.

 Alarm Bell

Replacing faulty equipment will cost money and can be avoided with careful maintenance.

Maintaining refrigeration

Fridges and freezers are used constantly to stock products so it's important to check them regularly for efficiency. You may want to buy breakdown cover to insure against unwanted surprises.

SETTING THE TEMPERATURE

Fridges and freezers should be set at appropriate temperatures. The coldest part of the fridge should be no more than +5°C and the freezer at –18°C or below. You may need to adjust the temperature dial on the fridge depending on the time of year to maintain these temperatures. Be careful not to leave doors open as this will allow heat to enter causing the temperature to rise. Fridges that are over packed with food are less capable of storing food properly as it can be difficult to keep temperature levels down.

DEFROSTING FREEZERS

When frost builds up in freezers they don't work as well, and so need to be defrosted. This should be done every time frost has built up and not left for a long time – regular maintenance will make the task easier. When there is a depth of more than four centimeters of ice in the freezer you need to defrost it.

Defrosting will make the appliance more energy efficient and increase its storage capacity.

CLEANING

Fridges need to be cleaned out properly. The inside of fridges – the shelves and storage compartments – should be disinfected and cleaned thoroughly. External surfaces should be given the same treatment. Door seals, which usually get forgotten, need to be cleaned using a solution of detergent to remove any mould.

DISPOSING OF FRIDGES

Old fridges and freezers can damage the environment so when you need to dispose of them you must use the right method. Contact your local authority to see if your nearest recycling centre accepts them. Some will offer a collection service for a fee.

Summary

Any retail premises is vulnerable to burglary or vandalism so it is best to make it as secure as you can. The business has a lot of money invested into it and a surveillance camera reduces the risk of theft and crime. Keep on top of your energy management – failure to do so will only result in higher than needed costs. It is ideal to try and reduce your energy bills. Keeping the equipment serviced and maintained reduces the risk of it failing at a time when you need it most.

11
KEEPING THE BOOKS

Bookkeeping is the recording of all money that comes in and out. Every business, no matter how small, is required by law to record financial information. There are lots of computer spreadsheets available to help you record information – Excel for example. Or you can use pen and paper records.

If you are running your own business you will need to register with HM Revenue and Customs as self-employed. There are fines if you fail to register. You must also complete a self-assessment tax return every year and pay National Insurance contributions.

Keeping records

Keeping records of financial transactions is an important part of the business. It is a legal requirement for businesses to keep financial records and failure to do so will lead to problems later on. If you input information onto a computer from paper records, you should still keep a copy of the original as there are penalties for not keeping proper records to support a tax return or claim.

It really does not matter whether you use a computer software package or a simple pen and paper account book as long as you can keep information together. Make sure the system works for you.

Good record keeping will help because it:

☐ allows tax returns to be completed much more quickly

☐ allows the correct payment of tax

☐ helps manage the business and its budget

☐ can reduce accountancy fees as accurate information saves time

☐ can be used to support any claims.

KEEPING RECORDS UP TO DATE

Be sure to update your record regularly. HM Revenue and Customs can decide to look into your tax returns or claims whenever they choose. If they do so, they may want to view your records. It will save your time and theirs if you are able to show that the records kept are accurate and up to date. Failure to do so may result in a penalty.

Records should be kept for long periods of time because you never know when you need to look back at them. VAT-registered businesses need to keep records for at least six years.

In general, information needs to be kept for five years from the last day your return was filed.

It is good to make a habit of spending time each day recording and filing your records. If you're in business with a spouse/partner you could take turns to do the paperwork.

All money paid out that relates to the business needs to be recorded in detail. This includes payments on your business bank statements and other cash payments. Each transaction recorded should have the date of the transaction, a full description and the amount.

As this trade mostly deals in cash, and assuming a cash register is used, till rolls can also be kept to track sales, and these figures can be recorded in the books. You must also keep all invoices and receipts. This includes a record of all work-related transactions – receipts such as telephone bills, rent and utility bills must also be kept.

FINDING THE TIME TO DO PAPERWORK

Running a catering business is a hands-on job and it can take some discipline to sit down to do paperwork after a day preparing food and serving customers. But this is a very important aspect of the business and needs to be given as much effort as working in the premises.

Make sure you organise a suitable space that is quiet enough to work in, and be sure to have the necessary filing facilities for your paperwork so that it is organised and easy for you to find. Record-keeping can be done in the evening when you have finished your teatime shift or it can also be given some time if you close after 2pm for a short break. You could leave the work until your day off (usually Sunday) though doing it earlier in the week will save you using your time when you could be enjoying other activities.

TOP TIP Find a good time to do your paperwork and make it a habit to record and update records.

I usually attend to these tasks during a set hour in the evening. During this hour, my full attention is on sorting and updating records as I find it can get confusing if the work is left too late. If an evening has been particularly busy I leave it to the next day but I find that spending most evenings doing some work is better than finding I have a huge amount to do later.

MAKING SURE BOTH PARTNERS CAN DO PAPERWORK

I find that the person who normally handles record-keeping tasks is much more efficient at doing them well, which can lead to complications when someone else takes over the role. In order to avoid future problems, the individual who deals with this task should train other partners in the business, so that the work can be taken over when they are unavailable.

Recording information

I record my turnover and expenses on a weekly basis on a worksheet that is printed off the computer.

The typical weekly worksheet below shows what money is going into the business and what is going out.

Goods purchased	Amount	Takings	Amount
Potatoes		Monday	
Fish		Tuesday	
Buns		Wednesday	
Sausages		Thursday	
Food supplier/ and other items		Friday	
		Saturday	

Week's total:

Other payments	Amount
Self	
Wife/husband	
Employees	
Gas/Electricity	
Rent/mortgage	
Rates/water rates	
Insurance	
Cleaning materials	
Telephone	
Oil/fat	
Cash drawings	

Using an accountant

Even if your business is relatively small you will probably need an accountant to produce the accounts (based on the information you give them). An accountant can also deal with your personal tax, and minimise the tax you need to pay, so it is important to give them sufficient details of your business accounts. They will need full details on the income and expenses of the business and all your records to ensure the figures add up.

 You must know the dates you need to submit tax returns and make sure your accountant has received all the necessary details before these deadlines.

How much an accountant charges depends on how much time they spend. The more accurate and up-to-date your accounts are, the less time it will take the accountant and the less expensive their charges will be. It is also a good idea to seek advice from your accountant on the best way to keep and record information.

Profit and loss account

Your accountant will produce a profit and loss account after receiving all the necessary details. This account shows how well the business has traded over a period of time (usually the last six months or year). It basically shows how much the business has earned and how much it has paid out in costs such as wages, production costs and so on.

Sometimes referred as a 'P&L', it starts with the gross income – the total of all money that comes in from sales – and takes away cost of sales to calculate the gross profit. Then it takes away overheads (sometimes called fixed costs). These include the rent for your premises, marketing costs, wages, telephone, gas and electricity, insurance and so on. That will give the operating profit. Add any other income and take away any other expenses and that will give you the net profit before tax.

A TYPICAL PROFIT AND LOSS ACCOUNT

Sales

Gross profit (achieved by taking away cost of sales)
Equals gross profit

Minus expenditure

Telephone
Advertisng
Cleaning supplies
Rates
Insurance
Accountancy
Gas
Electric
Wages
Miscellaneous
Rent/mortgage

Depreciation
Fixture and fittings

Profit before tax (net profit)

For the profit and loss account to be produced, you need to provide the accountant with all the relevant and accurate information. This means that all sales and expenses in the business need to be recorded to ensure accuracy.

Balance sheet

This statement displays the financial situation of a business at a certain time, usually at the end of the financial year. It is a snapshot of the performance of the business and shows assets and liabilities. It is different from the profit and loss account which shows how the business achieved its financial status. The information in a balance sheet is useful in assessing the financial position of a business.

VAT (Value added tax)

If your sales exceed the current threshold of £67,000 then the business will need to register for VAT with the Inland Revenue, after which a record of all goods and services supplied or received must be kept. If the VAT from sales is more than the amount on purchases then the difference must be paid. However, if the VAT from sales is less than the figure from purchases then the difference can be claimed back from the Inland Revenue.

Record-keeping needs to be fully accurate and up-to-date as HM Revenue and Customs must be able to trace details of all transactions from your records. Be sure to keep and file all purchase invoices, till rolls and other documents. More information on VAT can be found by contacting Customs and Excise or on the website (www.hmrc.gov.uk/vat/index.htm).

Summary

Recording financial information is necessary in any business and time needs to be given to do it properly and not wait until paperwork piles up. You must be organised and disciplined with the paperwork duties, particularly if it is a part of the business you dislike. Claims and tax returns need to be backed up by your records. Also, if your business faces any tax investigations from the Inland Revenue your financial details need to be fully available and up-to-date.

12
TIPS OF THE TRADE

Controlling portion size

Portion size can be a challenge as the customer wants value for money. It is important to train staff so that the sizes of portions, especially of chips, are the same every time – and not too big or too small.

The best way to control portion sizes is to use food trays, that way the portion sizes of orders such as chip meals will automatically be controlled. There is only so much food you can put on a tray and be able to wrap it up neatly. Trays can come in different sizes. Use one that can control your portions but also allows value for money for the customer.

Use a serving tray and place a sheet of greaseproof paper on it. Put on enough chips to fill the tray, then slide the greaseproof paper onto the wrapping paper. This method not only controls the portion of your chips, it is also quicker than not using a tray.

If, however, you prefer not to use a tray to measure portion sizes, then be sure to know how many scoops of chips will make a portion and how many will produce a larger size. This speeds up the process so that it becomes mechanical and does not require too much thought.

Alarm Bell

Controlling your food portions must be done to stay in profit but you also need to give the customer value for money.

PUTTING FISH, CHIPS AND PEAS ON A TRAY

Place the chips on the tray evenly, and then the peas. Then put the fish on top as it will appear larger this way.

PORTION SIZE OF SAUCES

Use a standard way to put sauces on trays of chips, such as two scoops for a portion. Make sure that all staff are trained in these portion controls.

TESTING PORTION SIZES

You may want to serve yourself a portion of your food wrapped in paper so you can test the size. If you find that you cannot manage to eat all the food, the portion size may be too big. Or if you find you're still a little peckish afterwards, it may not be enough. You can try this out on family and friends too to see what they think.

PORTION SIZE AND PRICE

Your profits can be maximised when food portions are controlled. Of course, portion size must also allow value for money, but there is no point in serving sizes that are too large as the customer won't be able to eat it all.

On our menu we have small and large chips. For small, we charge £1.00. For large, £1.50. We also offer a 70p portion which is half the size of a small chips. I try to offer different sizes to accommodate the needs of the customer. This seems to work both in satisfying the customers and avoiding unnecessary food wastage.

Customers can be difficult to please, but in this business you are providing a food service, and their needs must be met. Different customers may of course have different opinions about how much they want. During a lunch opening, for example, builders and tradesmen may want a quick fix for lunch. Their portion sizes are usually controlled as many will ask for orders that are placed on trays. Another customer may be ordering for a family and would appreciate a larger quantity. Elderly customers generally do not like their portions too large.

Quality, quantity and value for money

The heading pretty much says all. Giving large portions that aren't up to scratch will not do it; the customer needs to see value for money in a decent-sized portion of really good quality.

QUALITY OF YOUR PRODUCT

The most successful businesses today are efficient and produce great results. In short, a company which practises the best quality controls will be successful.

If you want to stand out from your competitors the key is to compete in quality and to offer better value for money along with a friendly service. Mainly, it is the quality of your food that will bring customers back. This is because quality speaks for itself.

I do find it a challenge to get the food right every time but it is the same for every catering establishment. Producing quality food continuously needs constant effort, and the process of continuous improvement brings quality.

 Your service and staff all contribute to quality. The highest standard of quality is when your products and staff join forces to create a solid service.

KEEPING A CLOSE EYE

In many restaurants, the head chef will normally monitor every plate of food before it goes out to customers. If it is not up to standard, the food is usually binned. If you are running a small food outlet you should try to incorporate similar quality controls so that the food is perfect every time.

 When standards are high in food quality and service, people will travel far to get to your establishment.

I pay close attention to whatever goes out to customers. Your staff may not care as much about the standard of the food as you do. You can't really blame them – the business belongs to you and their job is mainly to perform a role to a good level during a shift. You are the one who must focus on the food. I know this is important, especially for my regular customers as they are the key people who allow the business to keep running.

Customers always notice when there is something wrong in quality. Giving good food to the customer must be the main priority of a catering establishment – if not you cannot expect to be in business for long.

Here are guidelines to help you avoid mistakes in this area:

☐ Always check to see chips are fresh and edible.

☐ Always test the freshness of fish and meats.

☐ Do not sell pies or pastries that are dry as a result of being left too long in the display cabinet.

☐ Always use fresh lettuce and salad – do not use any salad that has changed in colour.

☐ Aim to make fresh gravy and sauces daily.

☐ Refuse to sell anything but the freshest food to the customer.

☐ Throw away any food that is not up to standard.

It is sometimes impossible to keep an eye on everything that goes out of the shop when in service. Staff must be informed of the importance of giving the customer quality food and if they notice anything wrong, they should let you know.

Consistency

Probably the most challenging thing for any food establishment is to be able to make consistently good food all the time. It must be done every day and kept up through the hours in service. Whether you're a pianist, an athlete or in this case providing a fast-food service, being great sometimes is not enough. What matters is how good you are all the time.

CONSISTENCY OF FOOD

A customer who comes in to buy a portion of chips and fish and orders it again the next week should receive the same quality and size as the week before. For example, the batter should always be the same thickness, not sometimes more watery or thicker than usual.

Alarm Bell

To keep the same standard of food consistently takes skill.

Above all, the quality has to be maintained on all food products because it is the primary reason the customer returns. Being consistent is no easy task and in a small catering outlet the responsibility to turn out good consistent food is down to one person – you.

To be consistent you need to:

☐ Be prepared and always on the ball.

☐ Never cut corners as it will affect the end result, the product.

☐ Be consistent in all areas of preparation.

☐ Get enough rest after opening hours so that you can put more energy into the work.

☐ Use the same ingredients – the same potatoes and fish, burgers and other food items and not change anything unless it needs to be improved.

☐ Keep the level of oil the same so that it turns out food the same every time.

CONSISTENCY OF SERVICE

As well as ensuring the consistency of the food you need to make sure that other aspects of the business are consistent:

☐ Good communication with employees.

☐ Employees who perform well in service.

☐ Friendliness to customers and regular rapport-building.

☐ Advertising and promoting the business.

EVERY AREA COUNTS

All areas of the business must be consistent to maintain a high standard. The truth is, if even one small area is neglected it will break your 'standard' chain which will ultimately affect the business. I find that in operating the business everything has to be thorough – preparing and cooking, having good customer rapport, regular advertising and managing employees well. All these things need to be done consistently and in harmony to enable the business to see results. Developing and executing consistency has been one of the secrets of many successful fast-food chains.

 In a food business, consistency is king.

Managing your own premises means you need to work on everything. We always try to manage staff the best we can and work hard to make sure all food that leaves the premises is produced reasonably quickly and is good and consistent. We then give attention to stock deliveries to see if there has been a reduction in quality. On top of that we try to always maintain hygiene and keep the premises looking inviting.

USING SYSTEMS TO ENSURE CONSISTENCY

In my first year in business, I made sure I sat down once a month to review each area in the business to spot any issues there might be with consistency. I found those issues were mostly related to the products and staff performance. Preparation procedures needed to be constantly monitored to make sure that there was consistent quality in the food.

The way I finally remedied the problem was to have set systems in place. Now, all preparing and operating in the premises is done to the minute and to the second. Using a set time in doing things minimises chances of inconsistency and helps achieve the required results. I have a set time to start my work every day, a time to turn on equipment and also accurate times in preparation. The set times and procedures are used throughout the day until closing time.

Having such procedures and systems in place can ensure consistency and also gives you the confidence that you are sure the customer is getting consistently good products.

Managing and monitoring staff

Staff must be managed properly and monitored at all times. Your ability to manage is key when controlling the staff and their work. Some of my staff are very good at their job, but there are others who at times are not up to scratch in their performance. This can cause customer dissatisfaction and affect the operation.

The breakthrough came for me in realising that when there is an issue over the performance of employees it has a direct link with me as the manager. As a result I direct more attention to employees who need to improve their performance. The results have improved significantly, but to maintain this requires consistent monitoring and managing of staff.

We have some members of staff who know the operation well and they help to manage part-time workers. They will do most of the serving while part-time staff take orders and put those orders into bags. Giving experienced staff more responsibility and having other workers support them seems to work, which in turn helps the working and management of staff.

Always use good ingredients

During our early days in business we spent a lot of time sourcing the right stock and ingredients. We knew it was important for the customers who use our service. Without the right ingredients, there will be limits to your success.

So when the right stock is sourced and customers are content with it, try not to change it unless it can be replaced with something better.

There will be times when you are tempted to cut back on costs by using less expensive products. Try not to use ingredients that are unreliable or cheap in order to save costs. When making fish and chips, the right potatoes need to be used along with preferably fresh fish, fried with a well-selected batter. The frying medium used should be top notch. It is important to be thorough in preparation and in choosing the best ingredients because if you do not it will show in the food.

 Remember that quality ingredients equal great foods.

Every step of the preparation process will affect the end product and the ingredients are key. Your food is your product and well-chosen stock will guarantee a good-quality end product. Everything you use to put a product together should be thought about. The salad used in burgers should be fresh and washed before serving. The buns need to be fresh and any that are hard should not be used. You cannot have one ingredient with quality and another without.

Always give the customer hot food

Try to give the customer the hottest food possible. This may be obvious but you will be surprised how often something like this can be overlooked. Giving customers food that is not warm enough does happen and is not acceptable. It is mostly the fault of poor preparation or simply a careless mistake.

Running a food establishment is not a walk in the park. Thoroughness is needed throughout the whole operation for it to be successful. Being able to deliver hot food to the customer all the time is again down to strict quality controls. You need to monitor the operation and be sure that all the food in display cabinets is kept warm.

Ensuring the food given to your customers is hot enough relies on your skills in preparing food and being able to maintain its heat. Be extra careful when heating food up in microwave ovens – be sure that the food is given enough heating time and is hot enough to sell. Food can be tested for heat levels using a thermometer.

Putting up prices

As gas and electricity prices increase and stock supplies in the business follow suit, you will have to raise the prices of the products you are selling. I mentioned earlier in the book that I think the price of fish and chips is too low. All the fish and chip shop owners who charge too little should unite and raise their prices to help the industry.

Prices should be reviewed once every two to three years, and rises implemented early in the year for people to get used to them.

White sea-fish is not a cheap food supply and its expense is increasing. Selling it too cheaply can only devalue the product making it difficult to make a decent margin. Customers are less likely to moan about price increases if they're getting a quality product.

You may also want to find out what prices are charged in other outlets in the area. This will give you an idea of how much to put your prices up by. In areas where there are issues such as unemployment it can be difficult to raise prices, but prices on all products should be set to make a profit. Think about each product sold and work out how much it costs to stock and prepare it. This will be different for each product. You may be selling some products at bargain prices that can be raised. However, some products that sell well may be less popular after a price rise.

I try to create a balance of pricing on products. For example, fish and chips must make a good profit as they involve a lot of preparation. Other products, for example small sausages and fishcakes, can be priced more cheaply so that people will have a choice of price range. I find that this supports the business and keeps people coming back. So we maximise the price on whatever takes a lot of preparation and offer other products at a lower price to encourage people to return to our shop.

Alarm Bell

If you have just bought an outlet don't raise the prices yet. It is important to get established first.

Improving the service

Don't forget to improve your product and service when you raise your prices. Aim to give the customer more for their money. It is important to raise the standard of quality, which means sourcing better ingredients for the product, whilst also improving the service and not just raising the price. Giving more to the customer in terms of quality creates more value in your product. Try to involve staff and ask them to contribute their opinions and ideas.

The last time I raised my prices, I focused on improving the service which included:

☐ Changing the frying fat to one that was more efficient.

☐ Changing the batter to an organic version which contains anti-oxidants and beneficial minerals.

☐ Carrying out a staff evaluation to improve their performance.

☐ Finding ways to improve all aspects of the food preparation process.

☐ Assessing the business operation as a whole to find out what needed to be worked on.

☐ Adding new and interesting products to the menu.

It can be helpful to evaluate the service of others to get a clear picture of their strengths and weaknesses. Knowing and educating yourself more about other local food businesses can help improve and run your establishment.

Have a look at your local competitors and see what they are doing wrong. You may want to concentrate on what they don't have. Then improvise on what they are doing right. We have done this by matching some products that a nearby food business was selling a lot of. Giving more will also give a good first impression to new customers and mean that you are able to retain your existing client base.

Alarm Bell

Customers are always looking for higher standards and food retailers must keep pace to trade in this market.

Improving the standards of the business includes evaluating yourself and your performance. As you are the key decision-maker you need to assess if your performance has been sound. See what you need to work on, and you will be able to raise the standard higher since the business will be likely to change with you.

Staff standards

Apart from improving the food and ingredients, it is important to also look at the performance of individual staff. If an employee has been more of a hindrance than an asset, it may be wise to find a replacement. Some people you hire may be very suited to this type of work and you may soon find that they need very little supervision. Others will function better with your management.

Alarm Bell

Part of your service will be delivered by your staff, so if one of them is not supporting the business, they are causing damage.

With other areas of the business to attend to, you may think it is difficult to always assess standards from staff. But you will be able to do it because you are working with them most of the time. Staff standards are maintained when they are under good management. I monitor and sense how the staff are doing and know when they are making an effort, or not.

We always knew that apart from food quality, the performance of our workers would play an important part in the quality of the overall service. This is because we cannot do everything in the premises by ourselves. If their performance is of a high standard, and continues to be so, it helps to support the business on an ongoing basis.

Customer service

Customer service needs to be great to keep customers happy. Things that customers think are important are:

☐ friendly staff

☐ product quality

☐ value for money.

Having excellent customer service can give you an edge over other retailers. It needs to be improved constantly, and maintained at a high level to ensure customer satisfaction and increase customer loyalty.

You must frequently ask yourself, 'How am I doing?' in terms of good customer service. Be honest and understand there is always room for improvement. You should always try to improve the standard of service.

Repeat business is built by the quality of your product and service and the way customers are treated.

The customer service of your establishment should be able to rival larger retailers. If not it must be worked on. We have always been satisfied by the customer service of one of the major supermarkets and we have tried to emulate their style. If your customer care is good it is likely that the people who use your service will come back.

Never forget that your customers are spending their cash in your premises and can easily go somewhere else that provides a better service.

Improving the décor

Some shops, for example, may need some cosmetic improvement to the interior or shop front. Even changes to the decoration of the premises can make a positive impact. Once there has been a renovation, people will notice the improvement, and it shows that you care about the business even at a cosmetic level. Just a new coat of paint will make a difference.

A few years ago, we decided to lay new flooring through the entire shop. We also thought the shop front needed a face lift, so we invested in new signage. It was a refreshing change and worth the investment. Customers liked the new look and people who had not been in before came in to try the food. Cosmetic improvements will certainly not hurt the business.

Getting feedback

Your existing customers are a good source of feedback for your service and its products. Customers may let you know what they think by commenting on your business. You may want to talk to them about what they think about the current service and what they would like to see improved. Some regular customers who have a good relationship with you may tell you about anything they think you're doing wrong, but if your customers are not telling you, just ask them.

Customers are usually glad to contribute feedback as it shows that you care about their needs and opinions, and they realise that you want to provide a better service for them.

Try to be direct and ask them for their opinions. If you do not like to ask directly you could leave comment forms on the counter for customers to fill in when they are waiting for their order. Customers may answer more honestly in writing and you can learn a lot about your business that way. If any issues come up, have them remedied or improved.

Once all feedback comments are collected see what issues need your attention. Find out what you're doing well and find out what needs to be worked on.

If your premises has tables and chairs for people to sit you can order a meal and have staff serve you, then assess what you like and don't like about the service.

Improving your menu

You may want to improve the menu by increasing your current product range. There should be innovation in this so do not be afraid to try some products out. It takes only a few customers to love the product for it to be successful. You may want to choose a product that you believe in and that is a proven success elsewhere and so likely to do well. Or you could take the initiative and go for a product that is unusual and different but which you think should be given a try.

Last year, I added a new fried chicken product to my menu. Though it was not selling as well as the burger products, there were some customers who tried it and now they order it every time they come in.

When launching a new product, stock small amounts of it at first and test it. See if there is a market for it from your premises and stock more only when there is some success.

You may want to add new products one at a time so that they are given time to blend into the menu. Give time for a new item to establish itself with customers and only then add another new product.

Fast-food businesses in general have been under some pressure to provide healthy food options. You may want to add some low-fat products to cater for people who are on a calorie-controlled diet or want to have fast food without the usual calories you would expect.

A delivery service

To further adapt to your customers' needs for convenience, you may want to offer a delivery service in your local area or within, for example, a five-mile radius. A driver can be hired or you could do the deliveries yourself as long as you have competent staff or a partner to be in charge of the premises while you are away.

In order for a delivery operation to be efficient, it must be quick and able to deliver food hot. Hire someone who knows the local area well or if you are going to do deliveries yourself be sure you are familiar with the area. Invest in a road map of the town or city you're in. For greater efficiency in finding addresses you could use a GPS navigator.

Know what your timescale is for delivering the order. Of course this may depend on how busy the shop is and how many deliveries need to be done. A reasonably quick and general timescale would be 20–30 minutes.

Additional services

Part of your service could be to cater for functions or parties where you are able to deliver a large amount of food. You could provide free delivery for large size orders. We have customers who ask for a massive fish and chip order for special gatherings. We value their custom, give them the best the we have, and they like to use us again.

Know your customers personally

There are extras you can do to improve the business. As the owner you can try to get to know your customers more personally, to create a bond. Just as importantly, you must allow them to get to know you. The customers will appreciate it and it can raise the service to a whole new level. Be friendly, but not over confident or cocky. Get to know their names and do not be shy or too reserved as it can come across as being rude as customers feel you do not want to talk to them.

When you build solid relationships with your customers, it benefits both you and them.

When you get to know your regular customers well, they become friends. There will be a stronger rapport which encourages customer loyalty – they will be more likely to do business with you. You will be able to find out information from some close regular customers like their occupation and so on. Ask them how their family is doing and for updates on things they may have talked about. Building strong relationships with the people who come into your shop can gain you custom for a long period.

Common complaints

If a customer is unhappy about something they may complain. In this business it will usually be the food they complain about, and it is important to listen to what the customer says. Unless you get absolutely everything right from the start of business, you are bound to receive at least one complaint. When you are new to the trade there will inevitably be some lessons to learn.

Common complaints include the following:

☐ The food is cold.

☐ The food is off, or has caused customers to have food poisoning.

☐ The food is dry.

☐ The food is horrible.

☐ The service is poor.

Complaints can tell how your business is doing and it is critical that you listen to them and improve your service and/or food accordingly. Successful food businesses are likely to receive very few complaints because they have perfected the art of making good consistent food. If you receive more than a few complaints it shows that the business operation and standard is poor.

Most customers don't actually express their dissatisfaction, they just don't return to your premises. In fact, only a very small percentage of people will tell you if they are aren't happy with the service. Although there's nothing you can do about it, you can't know there is something wrong if people do not tell you. Consequently, when someone does speak up and complain they are actually doing your business a favour.

 It is very important to learn from complaints and not repeat the same mistakes over and over again.

DEALING WITH COMPLAINTS

Once you have received a complaint you should try to resolve it by dealing directly with the customer. If the complaint has come in a form of a letter, you may want to acknowledge it so that the sender knows you have received it. Apologise to the customer and offer to put things right.

Sometimes the customer should be refunded, but ask them whether the mistake can be corrected before giving their money back. Depending on the nature of the complaint, you may be able to offer to make the food again then and there – but be sure to make it good! It is much better to be able to correct the complaint by offering to put things right and giving them food that is up to standard.

Giving the customer good service will leave a positive impression but refunding them doesn't do anything for your reputation.

When dealing with a complaint, you should take full responsibility for the problem. Try not to be defensive. Be aware of the issues, then find ways to resolve them.

Refunds should generally be avoided unless customers ask. The best thing to do is to correct the problem instead of simply returning their money.

LEARNING FROM COMPLAINTS

When a complaint is received it tells you what is wrong with your establishment. The lesson must be learned and the problem must be corrected. I remember once a customer complained about our portions being too small. I took look at our sizes and agreed that they could do with increasing. I told him that we would sort it out and make the portions larger. He never complained again.

Know how to apologise when something goes wrong.

It's a good idea to create a complaints folder so that there is a record of each complaint with steps on what was done to resolve it. This folder can be looked at after a period of time or checked to see the amount of complaints received each year. This helps to monitor the performance of the business and highlights major issues. It also makes clear what must be improved.

The customer is always right

A business can exist only when there are people spending money in it. The business is there because of its customers. When running a service it is imperative to understand the importance of the customer – they should be respected because they are spending their hard-earned cash. You offer a food service in exchange for money and you want your customers to repeat the exchange.

 The customer may not always be right, but the customer should always win!

Staff need to be aware of the importance of the customer; every customer's satisfaction secures their jobs and your business. Issues with dissatisfied customers must be resolved and at no time should you argue with customers. They need to be viewed as the boss, which perfectly emphasises their importance.

Establishing good relationships with customers and clients is absolutely vital to your success. Most retailers depend on repeat business and this is definitely true for fast-food businesses. If your customers receive poor service it is unlikely they will come back. If the customer has a good experience the chances are high they will return.

Customers should be treated well and they should receive service with a smile. Try not to ignore people when they arrive (even when you're busy), and be sure to have a member of staff ready to take their order. If staff are busy, make time to do it yourself. Customers generally do not like to wait to be served.

 The customer keeps you in business.

Always remember to:

☐ provide excellent customer service

☐ give the customer more for what they're paying

☐ learn from any complaints from customers

☐ establish good relationships with customers.

LISTENING TO YOUR CUSTOMERS

Another thing to remember is always to listen to the customer. Sometimes people have specific requests – for example, you might receive an order which asks for chips that are browner than usual. Or a customer might request freshly-made chips – don't give them chips that have been par-fried. It's really important, as far as possible, to make the food the way the customer asks for it.

If there has been a complaint about a product, as discussed above, it should be looked at to see what the problem was and how it can be corrected. Anything that the customer comments on should be taken seriously and not ignored or forgotten.

If you understand your customers better, you are much more likely to be successful and increase your profits.

Listen to both your regular customers and to new customers so that each person who comes into your shop can be satisfied with the service. Try to understand your customers better because you are the one who will know their needs. Sometimes, for example, a customer will ask you if you can stock a certain product that they like. We had requests for a pie that one of our customers wanted to try which we didn't stock. I ordered some for the customer. Don't make a situation where someone has to go to another establishment for a product that you can find and stock.

Alarm Bell

Remember that your competitors are trying to get to your customers every day.

We generally like listening to customers, and they generally like to talk. Whether it's about our service, their holiday plans or what's happening in the world, we are glad to listen. It all helps to build rapport and provide good service.

Dealing with trouble

Antisocial behavior is a common problem for small shops including fast-food outlets, newsagents and grocery stores. One of the reasons is that many small shops are based in community areas which can make them vulnerable. Young people who engage in drinking, taking drugs and vandalising the neighbourhood can make life difficult. They usually drink on the streets because they are too young to drink in pubs.

Experience tells me it is not wise to confront troublesome teenagers, or to provoke them. I have found it is a good idea to give them some respect; you need to be respectful before you can expect someone to respect you. So before you go out and give them a big telling off, think about what might happen.

Your premises is vulnerable so in order to protect the business and the property, it is much better to avoid confrontation. Young people will spend money in the shop and their custom should be valued like anybody else's. If there is a group of youths standing outside the premises and affecting the business (such as obstructing other customers), explain this to them and ask them to move.

AVOID CONFRONTATION

As the owner of the shop you have the power to refuse certain individuals in the premises. However in my experience this should be avoided at all costs – it only provokes negative feelings and unwanted attention from people.

The best approach is to avoid confrontation as conflict may affect your running of the business. There could be times when you have to confront someone but do it in a calm and methodical way.

When dealing with difficult people you should:

- [ ] use their names if possible

- [ ] request their cooperation

- [ ] try to develop a positive relationship with them

- [ ] call the police only if it is absolutely necessary.

Getting through quiet periods

All businesses suffer periods that are quieter than they would like. These times can happen for a number of reasons.

- [ ] Market conditions may affect trade; job losses in the area can also have an effect on people's spending.

- [ ] The new year is traditionally a quiet time as many people spend a small fortune at Christmas, so they are focused on repaying their credit card debts. After the biggest highlight (for most people) of the year, it usually takes some time for people to reorganise their finances. At the same time some people are still spending as many high street retailers reduce prices in their January sales.

☐ Over Christmas people usually overeat and over-indulge in alcohol consumption and this has a definite effect as people try not to eat so much fast food for a while.

All these reasons play a part in influencing business trade, but remember, all businesses have times throughout the year where sales are not up to target.

There are various ways to deal with quiet periods.

KEEP YOURSELF BUSY

I have found it is better to keep busy than to simply wait for business to arrive. You will find that there are many tasks around the premises that need to be done to keep the things running well. This includes preparing food, managing staff and monitoring stock. Keep yourself on the move and concentrate on running the business well.

You should always be thorough in your preparation, and this includes cleaning. The man who founded McDonald's, Ray Kroc said, 'If you have time to lean, you have time to clean'. Not only does it keep you busy but it makes the premises more hygienic and gives a fresh feeling to customers when they do come in. This keeps the momentum going and keeps you active which stops you from becoming bored.

It is also important to prepare foods – for example par-frying chips and checking to see whether the batter needs to be topped up. As business can sometimes be unpredictable, if a sudden rush of customers does come in it is best always to be prepared.

 As well as cleaning and preparing foods, keep an eye on your stock of food trays and other non-food items.

BE ALERT AND READY

Working people get a chance to eat only when their lunch break permits them. This is usually around 12pm – 1.30pm. People usually eat tea or dinner around 6pm – 7.30pm. Those are the times that you must be extra alert.

Outside these standard times business can be uncertain, but you must still be prepared. Be sure to have every product on your menu readily available. Do not think just because you sold lots of gravy yesterday, it will be the same today. It could be a curry day. Preparation to make sure you are on the ball is vital – remember that quiet periods are only temporary and thorough preparation is needed to serve people well.

When I have been to other fast-food places I have found some to be very inadequate and lacking in their preparation. These shops were not busy but found it overwhelming when they had a small rush of customers. It showed in their below-standard service and most of all in their product.

My advice is to do the necessary preparation in any quiet periods so that the standard of your food is kept high. Being alert for business means getting things ready so that when business arrives it will not be overwhelming.

MAINTAIN YOUR STANDARDS

Food businesses can lose their focus during quiet times. This can reduce the overall performance and their service is less impressive. Perseverance is needed to sustain standards. Even if you are suffering a quiet period, if your service and product quality is good then the trade should not take long to recover, as your standards will become your reputation.

 The trick is to try to satisfy every customer who uses your service.

When I notice a quiet time in the business, I know it is even more important to produce good food. When the business is doing well, you are being carried along by the momentum and the quality of the food will be generally consistent. In quiet times, it can be difficult to maintain these standards because of the unpredictability of whether the food will be sold or not. You find you have to work harder to deliver good standards of food to the customer.

Sometimes customers will go to try foods from a different food premises, but if the quality is not there they will always come back to you. If you make sure your standards are kept high, your customers will return.

When getting through a quiet period you should:

☐ Find the motivation to improve what you're doing.

☐ Remember to keep up the advertising and include special offers.

☐ Be patient and stay committed.

☐ Realise it can take some reasonable time for business to pick up.

☐ Keep present customers happy by maintaining high standards.

 During a quiet spell, try to keep your momentum going to deliver foods at high standards.

When you are selling food you need to focus on maintaining standards every day, and not just during quiet spells. If the quality of service is good most of the time, any market changes can be limited because your standards are high.

Dealing with the competition

All businesses face one unavoidable conflict – competition (how wonderful it would be if no one but you provided the service!). Competition should be taken very seriously. It is real, its effect is strong and it is not going to go away.

One way to look at competition is to view it as a reason for improving the business or quality of your product. It is important to stand out from the crowd and not be one more example of hundreds of other premises. Some people say that competition is healthy; to me it is simply a drastic need for improvement as competition affects my business!

Competition is the major reason that you should improve all aspects of the business and work on having a unique selling point.

To be unique, compared with the competition your business should have:

☐ more product choice

☐ products that are good value for money

☐ attractive and welcoming premises

☐ friendly staff

☐ higher quality

☐ higher standards.

The best businesses always offer something unique, something just that little bit better. You should aim for your service to be better than local competition, and to retain customers by rendering such a high-quality service that they do not want to visit another outlet.

PRODUCT CHOICE

Adopting a broader product range allows a business to diversify and grow. If you have multiple products for customers to choose from it can attract buyers with different preferences.

People like variety. Although fish and chips is widely eaten across the nation, it is only one product, so some traditional fish and chip shops have changed into outlets which specialise in other types of food as well. Pizzas and burgers, for example, are popular with children, while their parents can still have fish and chips.

Some innovation may be needed – some shops even sell a fish, chip and peas burger. (It consists of half a fish, a few chips and peas in a bun.) More and more traditional fish and chip shops are making their menus diverse by serving several types of fish. Most will sell burgers and some even add pizzas. They will usually change by renovating their shop and signage to show that they do not sell just fish and chips but also provide other food.

KEEPING STANDARDS IN NEW PRODUCTS

Each new product added to the menu should be as good as the fish and chips you sell. Some shops choose to stock a large range of products to keep up with customers' demands for variety by adding many new products such as pizzas and other products. Although variety is a bonus for food businesses it works only if you have the same high standard in every product.

 Spend time practising the preparation of new products.

You will have plenty of practice serving your main products, but new menu additions take some practice to prepare them well. Premises that specialise in fried fish and chips may find it a challenge to work with other foods they're not used to, and find it hard to bring them up to standard. This may even have an effect on their main products.

On one occasion we chose to try a new fried rib product. It was not as popular as fish and chips or burgers, and we found that the product browned too easily when it was fried. We could not reach a good standard so we later chose to take it off the menu.

Stock up on Good Friday

On Good Friday, part of the long Easter weekend, people who are Catholics tend not to eat meat but fish. It is generally busy on this day. Make sure you have plenty of fish and top up everything else, especially peas. Some shops are busy on the Thursday before Good Friday but this will depend on the individual premises.

Be prepared for winter

The winter in this country is longer than the summer, and people tend to eat more during the cold season. You may want to plan your first winter in trading so that nothing gets overlooked. Instead of relying on trial and error aim to get the first winter season as right as you possibly can.

STOCK UP

Be sure to stock up on supplies during this busy time of year. Many shops are busy during this time of year and it is better to be prepared; it is essential to stock up on everything.

Fish supplies will be at their most expensive because of demand. A way to avoid the high prices is to freeze a few stones of fish before the arrival of the inflated prices. Potatoes, however, are very difficult to stock in bulk because of limited storage space in a premises, so paying ridiculously high prices per bag of potatoes in December is unavoidable.

After running the business for a couple of years, you will have a good idea of what the business is like through that time of year and can adjust the stock levels to your expected business.

Alarm Bell

Suppliers will also be closed for a period of time in the festive season so you must have enough stock to continue until early January.

CUSTOMER SERVICE

Apart from stocking up, you will need enough staff through this period. It is important to have loyal staff to support the business through the busy time. This time of year is crucial in keeping existing customers satisfied and there will usually be new customers who try the service. I find that keeping the regulars happy means that they return in the new year, and so do new customers if they are satisfied with the service.

 During December I like to give my regular customers a card and a bottle of wine. The regular customer base is loyal and keeps us in business.

A Christmas tip box can be put on the shop counter and the cash can be shared out among staff. Staff like these bonuses and it keeps them happy. It is a great way to say thank you as they work so hard at this time of year.

Summary

This chapter has looked at the standards you need to maintain in your premises, and how to avoid some common pitfalls and be better prepared for the trade. You will find that once you have spent some time running an establishment, you will probably come across all the points discussed in this chapter. How well the operation runs will depend on the key points of consistency, quality and customer care, and your ability to find ways to raise the standards of service. You need to prepare sufficiently for different periods throughout the year.

13
TO TRANSFER OR TO EXPAND?

Selling the business

There may be a day when you will be ready to sell the business. I have known people who were in the business for 30 years, and loved doing what they did, but sold when they could no longer cope with running an outlet. Others realised that running a fast-food establishment was not meant for them.

Some people pass on the business to their children who can do well as the business is established and they have an experienced mentor to guide them. If the business is a freehold tenure, you may want to lease it out for a weekly income instead of selling the property and that you can then pursue other careers or interests.

PLANNING AHEAD

Try to plan ahead when selling, such as for the next two to five years. You should keep an eye on the performance of the general economy as it can affect the demand and price you will get for your premises. In market crisis conditions such as increasing interest rates or house-price falls people will be less able to borrow money because banks will have tighter lending controls. This will result in fewer potential buyers so it is favourable to sell when general market conditions recover. The best time to sell is when the market is healthy and people are buying. In a strong or rising market, you will be able to sell your business at a higher price.

 It makes sense to target your advertising in spring or summer instead of putting out adverts during the cold season when there are fewer businesses sold.

PREPARING THE FINANCES

Your turnover will always be one of the main interests for the buyer so it is important that you prepare up-to-date financial statements to reflect the performance of your business. Potential buyers will make their own judgements as to whether the business will be profitable in the future, as well as analysing the current financial status.

You should be able to provide financial statements for at least the last three years – preferably the last five. A business that has hit targets and increased its trade over the last three years is attractive to buyers.

 Most people want to buy a business that is already doing well and not have to build up the business themselves.

Your accounts should be able to prove the business turnover to buyers. Remember – it is not what you say but what you can prove. Be sure to have necessary accounts to back up your claims.

Sometimes people will ask for audited accounts, and although small businesses do not legally need to provide them, you will be seen as much more dependable if you have them. You will, however, need to provide accounts prepared by an accountant to enable the purchaser to borrow money. Lenders will accept accounts produced and checked only by an accountant.

Using a business transfer broker

These days most businesses are sold through a broker. The broker finds potential buyers who are interested in a business like yours and arranges appointments for them to come and see the premises.

Business brokers can be found in public listings such as the *Yellow Pages*, trade magazines, newspapers and on the internet. They often advertise in newspapers and trade magazines.

They will have their own website, and may list your business on other businesses-for-sale sites. They also have access to their own database of registered contacts of people looking for a food premises.

A business broker will do the following:

☐ Advertise your business online as well as offline.

☐ Advertise for as long as it takes to sell.

☐ Have close contact with you while you run your business without distractions.

☐ Develop links with interested parties.

☐ Negotiate with buyers on your behalf.

When you use a business transfer agency they will first send somebody to value your business. They then will have a talk with you regarding the agreement with them and their commission fee. This is usually high – around three per cent plus VAT – but can vary. Some agencies charge upfront fees for their advertising – have a look around at the deals that different brokers offer to decide if that is something you want to do.

Once you are happy with the agreement, a contract will be drawn up between you and the agency. Do read the terms and conditions of the contract carefully.

ADVANTAGES OF USING AN AGENCY

Potential buyers may feel more at ease speaking to a broker, and you may prefer not to deal with the buyer on your own.

Having a broker to deal with people who are interested allows you the time you need to continue running your business.

Brokers understand that it is important to be discreet, and so their general methods usually help you escape any difficulties or issues that would arise if customers and suppliers knew you were planning to sell. Not only that, customers knowing you want to sell can affect your trading.

Business transfer agencies are able to find people to view the business reasonably quickly and will contact you when someone is interested. They give you ongoing advertising until the business sells and will be able to reach more potential buyers than if you were to sell the business yourself.

DISADVANTAGES OF USING AN AGENCY

Some agencies are better than others – some will be able to find many people to view your business whilst another may not be able to generate any interest over a reasonable period of time. You will need to be sure that you are picking a good agency. In addition, agency commission fees are high and you can save a considerable amount of money if you do the work yourself.

RELATIONSHIP WITH BUYERS

Although an agency will negotiate for your interests, you may also need to deal with your buyer and answer any questions they have about the business. You do normally need to have a relationship with the buyer to enable the transaction to go smoothly and to solve any issues which arise during the selling process.

HAVE A BOTTOM LINE ON PRICE

Usually, the agency will contact you to give you an update on the progress of selling your premises. If it hasn't generated much interest they may offer feedback on why they think that is so.

They may suggest that your asking price is too high and ask if you would consider reducing the price to increase interest. If you feel the price is reasonable for the current market, then the price should not be reduced. However, taking a substantial amount off can make a real difference. It's important to have in mind a minimum amount that you would sell for, and try to reduce the price according to it.

 Don't reduce the price too much – just enough to allow some interest without hitting your bottom line.

Selling the business yourself

If you do not want to pay agency commission fees then you could sell the business yourself. This can be tough as you will not have access to a database of people to contact and will have to do all the advertising yourself. You never know how long it will take to sell and you will need to keep paying advertising costs until you find a buyer.

It is also unlikely you will be able to do the same level of advertising as a business broker, and so you will generate fewer leads. You will also be responsible for all parts of the sale process, including negotiation. It takes persistence and some time to attract somebody who wants to view the premises.

 When selling the business yourself, you are trying to save the costs of agency fees. You should decide how much you are prepared to spend on advertising and set yourself a budget.

NEWSPAPER ADVERTS

An advert can be placed in the business-for-sale sections of local newspapers. The costs will depend on how big the newspaper is – if you put an advert in a paper that covers a large region it can be expensive and it does not guarantee creating any interest. Advertising in local newspapers may draw interest from people wanting a similar business or people already in the trade wanting to expand. Bear in mind that some of the people who respond to your adverts may well be time-wasters.

ON THE INTERNET

You can list your business on a business-for-sale website for a fee. An online classified advert will usually run for a fixed period of time. Once the expiry date for the advert is due, if you have not yet sold your business, you will have to pay to renew the ad.

Other sites will charge in different ways. Some charge a monthly fixed fee to list your business. Some do not charge any fees in the beginning, but only when there is a potential buyer or lead.

 Most sites allow you to create and edit your advertisement online and include photographs.

Listing your business for sale online will reach lots of people, but the internet is crowded with many websites that offer the same service, so there is no guarantee that one business-for-sale site will reach the same level of potential buyers as a newspaper advert. If you do decide to advertise your business online it may be better to go with one of the more popular websites in order to be sure of hitting a larger target audience.

When selling a business yourself you need to do the following:

☐ Create interest by word-of-mouth – you could try letting people know that you intend to sell to see if anyone may be interested in purchasing a food business.

☐ Advertise in newspapers and on the internet.

☐ Be patient – know that it will sell in the end, and that it takes time to find a buyer.

❑ Realise that you need to be flexible when it comes to negotiating.

❑ Before a viewing, make sure the premises is clean in order to make a good first impression (this applies to viewings through an agency too).

❑ If there has been no interest after some reasonable time, consider reviewing the asking price. Assess if it is a reasonable amount to ask for in terms of the current turnover.

Showing people around

When people come to view the business show them around and be confident and helpful as you tell them about each area of the premises. You never know who will be interested. Some may seem to be interested in your premises and ask you for more information, but then you won't hear from them again. Others may genuinely like the business, but cannot raise the necessary finances.

 Make sure the premises look clean so that first impressions are good.

Talk a lot about the working equipment and its uses. Think about who you're talking to and adjust the information you give them accordingly – some people will have never had any experience working in a fast-food business, whereas others may already be running their own establishment and have decided to expand.

BE PREPARED TO ANSWER QUESTIONS

If you have had experience in selling a property you will find that it is similar, except that as it is a business sale there will be more questions asked.

When potential buyers come to visit your premises you should be able to answer any questions they ask. You may want to refer to chapter 2 – the queries we looked at when you're interested in buying a business may well be the questions you will answer when you are selling.

It helps to prepare yourself so that you know exactly how to handle each question asked. One of the most common questions is 'Why are you selling the business?' It is best to answer truthfully to avoid complications.

HOW LONG WILL IT TAKE TO SELL?

This very much depends on the asking price for the business. Other factors that affect selling include:

☐ location

☐ parking

☐ whether it is leasehold or freehold

☐ turnover.

The amount of time it takes to sell a business varies, but there are plenty of people looking to buy a business. These people may be first timers in the business who are looking for a career change, or people who have taken a break from the trade and want to re-enter. There are also people who want to buy a food premises and turn it into a different type of food outlet.

The most common reason for a slow sale is the asking price. If the price you're asking doesn't correlate with its turnover or property value then you may want to revise it.

Expanding

You can expand your operation by increasing sales and turnover, or by opening an additional branch. Expansion is a very brave decision so you need to be sure about the direction you are heading in.

The main reasons for starting another branch are:

☐ to start a chain

☐ to generate more income

☐ to eliminate competition

☐ because business is so good there is no reason not to expand.

Opening up a new business within the same area as your existing premises is a good tactic to reduce the local competition and to gain more market share. The more outlets you have, the larger the effect will be.

Some things you should consider before venturing into expansion:

☐ Expanding the business means building another successful outlet and all the risks that apply to the first premises will apply to the new premises.

☐ The work will double because of a second outlet.

☐ Can the current business operate well without you?

☐ Are you aware of the risks of starting another food outlet?

☐ Are you willing to sacrifice your personal time by putting your energy into another outlet?

You will need to decide whether expanding is for you. There is increased risk and a lot on the line – not least increased pressure and more sacrifice of your time. The work increases as businesses grow and expand.

Your experience in the industry means you should be able to apply your knowledge to the new premises.

It normally takes roughly the same amount of time to establish your second outlet as it did your first. Also bear in mind that just because your current business has been a success does not guarantee the same will happen when you start another premises.

RAISING FUNDS

In order to grow a small business you will probably need to raise some finances. You may want to take on a partner, or approach lenders. You have to assess your position and be careful not to overstretch yourself. If you don't evaluate the situation properly, and things go wrong with the new business, you could have a crisis on your hands.

The burden of repayments to lenders on two premises will be great, but the risks can be reduced by early planning and having a realistic look at your situation. Take the necessary time to evaluate your expansion ambitions until you are confident that it will give you the return on your investment that you need.

WHEN TO EXPAND

When exactly to expand the business can be a problem. You may want to assess the current market for your type of outlet, to see if the area you plan to expand in would welcome your food service. You should also ask yourself if you are ready to expand. Have you been in the business long enough to fully understand the industry and market? Are you competent enough with the necessary skills and knowledge for expansion?

If you are at all unsure you may want to re-think and wait until you feel fully capable.

Another issue that affects the time it takes to open a new branch is the performance of your existing business. Can anything be improved? You will apply the management principles used in the current business to the new premises. Usually it can be only as good as the first one so it's important to make sure that standards in the first one are as high as they can be.

Sit down with your spouse or business partner and plan your expansion goals. See if your targets are achievable and if it is the right time to pursue expansion. Your timing will play a major part in whether it succeeds, so choosing the right time to do it should be calculated through proper planning.

Somebody we know expanded too quickly and it didn't work out. Managing two premises was overwhelming and he struggled with the second business. The business was later sold to someone else who was capable of managing it properly. When you decide to increase your market share through an additional outlet you have to do everything you can to get it right.

CHECKING YOUR CURRENT BUSINESS

In order to make the second business successful, the first one should be perfect. Have a look at the trading accounts for the last three to five years to see how it has progressed. It is important to be sure that the current business is working perfectly and that the customers are happy. It is also useful to monitor and analyse any complaints made in the last twelve months. The results from your findings should have an effect on your decision about expansion.

As you can see, how your current business is performing affects the timing of expansion. Expanding too quickly by spreading the focus of your efforts on two individual premises may in the end affect the overall performance of both businesses.

You can run these checks on your business:

☐ Evaluate if your sales have increased since your first year of trading.

☐ Are your customers satisfied?

☐ Are your staff performing to the best of their ability?

☐ Does your management style need any improvement?

☐ Is your service the best it can be?

If your current business has fully passed all your checks then you could consider your options for expansion.

STAFFING COSTS

Another issue in expansion is the cost of the staff that you must employ to operate an additional premises. The potential turnover needs to be able to cover staff and other running costs.

If you are in business with a partner or spouse you can each take on one of the premises which will ease some of the pressure. If you need one of the premises to be run entirely by staff it will be expensive, which makes it even more crucial for the turnover of the business to cover all costs and be able to generate a profit.

 The staff will be key in the operation and they will have to be well trained and be reliable.

Recruiting employees for the new premises may take more time and planning than usual. You need to hire people who will support the new business. It is advisable to hire people who have had quite a lot of experience in the trade, who require no training and do not need much supervision. Very competent staff could cost you more money but may be much more reliable and able to make the new business a success.

CHOOSING A LOCATION

The exact location of the new premises must be thought through just as carefully as the first premises. As a lot of effort was used in establishing your current business, and you must try to reduce any risks of expansion failure. Spend weeks or months researching the location if need be. Effective expansion comes from planning thoroughly and not hastily rushing in.

You may want to open another premises close to your existing business to gain more market share of the area. You will be more familiar with the area you're in and that knowledge can reduce risks. Or you can set your sights on other areas that would benefit from your service, although assessing those areas will take more time.

REVISING YOUR BUSINESS PLAN

The business plan that you developed to open your existing business can be reviewed and re-written or modified to reflect your aim for expansion. As mentioned in the earlier section on buying a business, a well-written business plan clearly defines your goals and acts as a road map. A detailed plan can also act as an evaluation tool to spot any potential issues and weaknesses.

 Plan your expansion even more thoroughly than you did your first premises.

STARTING A NEW PREMISES

Starting a new premises will involve:

☐ working hard and spending time getting ready for the launch

☐ training up staff in the new premises

☐ juggling the two businesses to maintain standards

☐ being able to work on the new premises until it gets established.

If you have acquired an existing business it will already have its own turnover, which you can maintain and improve. You may want to make some cosmetic improvements to the interior of the premises or to change the name of the business. It is up to you to decide whether the new premises will operate as it did with the previous owners or whether it will sell exactly the same products and adopt the same operations as your existing business.

Your current business may need to act as a source of support until the new premises has time to establish itself with you as the new owner. Owning your own chain of outlets is like being the president of your company, which carries much more responsibility.

You have to make sure that your current business can run well without your supervision when you start up another branch.

One of the most difficult things about opening an additional business is finding the right people to manage your current premises. Ideally you need to recruit a manager whom you can trust to handle the affairs and operations of your existing business. This person must be capable of taking your place while you're away and knowing the business almost as well as you do.

Starting a chain

You would be dreaming if you thought you could emulate any of the major fast-food chains. Those chains started early on when there was very little or no competition and have been trading for decades. What you can do on a much smaller scale is to run a small chain.

The usual route to building a chain is to buy a similar business and implement your business principles and operating style in those premises, or to buy a shop premises and convert it into a food business.

A chain usually develops by acquiring one business at a time. Once an existing business is managed correctly with the right management and employees then another premises can be started, and the process repeated. Creating a chain can take a long time as the existing businesses need to be performing to their full potential before you attempt to open another branch.

Branding and style

A brand is a name, logo or slogan and its design displays the identity or essence of its company, product or service. One key objective of creating a brand is to forge a relationship with the customer so that they will use your service over another.

You can give your chain of outlets the same name to create a brand and its own identity.

Branding a small- or medium-sized business follows the same procedures and principles of branding larger retailers. The only difference is that smaller businesses will have a smaller market and reach, compared with larger brands. You can hire an interior designer so that each outlet in the chain has the same feel and style. The products offered will normally be the same in every outlet and when advertising is carried out, it should be scheduled at the same time for each branch.

You must spend a lot of time planning when starting your own chain, and you should think about what you want your organisation to be like – for example do you want to be known for providing a wide range of products? Perhaps you are keen to have a very modern shop layout. Making your service and business image fresh will benefit your brand-building and can differentiate you from other fish and chip shops.

BRAND NAME

The brand name is an ingredient of a trademark that identifies the brand owner as a deliverer of certain products or services. As a brand owner you can protect your proprietary rights through trademark registration.

A brand name should:

☐ be attractive

☐ be easy to pronounce and remember

☐ be easy to translate into other languages for its use

☐ be easy to recognise

☐ be able to attract attention and stand out

☐ suggest the product image and company.

ADVANTAGES OF BRANDING

A brand can usually command higher prices for its products – when there are two identical products, one which is branded and one which isn't, customers tend to think that the branded one is better – this is often because of its reputation and 'brand promise'. Brand promise is a statement expressed in a tag line – for example, 'The food we sell is the best in town.'

Another feature of brand promise is the core identity and character of the company.

A marketed brand can encourage trust from people which gives it an advantage over independent businesses.

Marketing techniques are used in branding to influence buying behaviour and to create a strong desire for the service. A particular brand can give the illusion that its products are much better than others. This is achieved through marketing strategies that are used to build the brand so that the name or logo is recognised.

DISADVANTAGES OF BRANDING

There are costs involved in the creating of a brand image or logo which will become relatively large for a small business. Maintaining a strong brand can involve a lot of marketing fees because people have to be exposed to the brand which requires a lot of advertising and will cost a lot of money.

Relying on word-of-mouth will save you money, but will also greatly slow down the exposure your brand receives. Also the ability to deal on a personal basis with customers is a unique advantage small businesses have over larger retailers. If your creation of a brand is ineffective it could give customers the impression that your establishment is losing its personal touch.

A brand has an image for people and it projects what products or services you sell. If you are known for selling just one main product, and you want to sell other products, will it work?

Establishing a brand usually takes a long period of time. For branding to work well it needs to incorporate extremely strong marketing and attack the market in all the right ways.

Point of sale systems

When you are increasing your premises you may want to look into installing POS (point of sale) systems which you can see in most retailers. They are increasingly used in the restaurant and catering industry for their accuracy and support in improving service efficiency.

Point of sales systems are computerised system registers that have taken over from conventional cash registers. They use touch screen technology and are linked to a network. They allow order entry and are able to keep track of sales and payrolls, and even generate accounting records. As orders are processed more quickly, service time is reduced and efficiency increased.

POS systems can record all sales and track the time of each transaction.

Advanced registers often have an all-in-one system which acts as a cash register, barcode scanner and credit/debit card terminal. Different options are available and can be customised for every business.

Since POS systems can keep such accurate records it combats theft much more effectively than using conventional cash registers. You can also ensure that every item is sold at the right price. Modern POS systems can give useful information about your business such as your most profitable products and sales reports, and can manage the inventory much more effectively.

ADVANTAGES OF A POINT OF SALE SYSTEMS

☐ Manages employees when the owner is not in the premises using its automating host functions. This keeps control of staff and maintains customer service levels.

☐ There is no need for calculating or checking received orders thereby creating fewer errors.

☐ Errors can be pinpointed without the need to analyse cash register receipts.

☐ Keeps accurate records of inventory levels.

☐ If used in each outlet, they can enable the consistent pricing of products.

☐ Can store customer details and previous order history.

☐ Able to process orders more quickly, which means more attention can be given to customer service.

DISADVANTAGES OF POINT OF SALE SYSTEMS

☐ Expensive to set up and run.

☐ Need to be maintained and updated.

☐ Staff require more training.

In the future probably all food businesses both large and small will have a POS system installed. Their accuracy is second-to-none and they are very reliable.

We have friends who use one in their restaurant business, and they have had no problems with it and find it very useful. They never have to worry about mis-counting cash. They have also found that it is very accurate and convenient for order-taking as orders taken in the restaurant area can be sent to the kitchen electronically. Now there is no need for the staff to go to the kitchen to deliver orders which has speeded up the service and operation of the restaurant.

Summary

Only you will know when the time is right to sell your business. When that time comes, you need to decide how you will sell it. Many people use the services of a business broker so that the premises can reach more potential buyers, and there is also support during the selling process. You may decide to expand your business. This will prove to be a challenging decision and its success depends on careful planning and the ability to be able to manage more than one premises. If you decide to expand further into a small chain you will have to manage several outlets, which means hiring the right people to support the operation. You will need to decide whether to commit and be responsible for more than one premises.

AND FINALLY...

Running your own fast-food business is an energetic affair and can be very exciting. There is a lot of hard work but when you get it right, it is enjoyable. If you get it wrong, you will wonder what you have got yourself into. The work is plentiful in this trade as you already know, but if you enjoy it, it will seem less like work.

Only by running your premises with commitment, providing quality products and having well-trained employees will you be successful. You should always be working to improve and maintain the standards of your service, and your approach to customer care will have a long-lasting effect on your relationship with customers.

Eating is a daily necessity which makes food businesses different from other industries. It cannot go out of fashion. Fast food is a growing industry and seems to have no limits to its growth, but it faces what all businesses must confront – competition – which means that only the outlets with the right standards can compete.

APPENDIX

Industry contacts

Organisation that works to support fish and chip businesses in the UK	www.federationoffishfriers.co.uk 0113 230 7044
Authority that works to sustain and raise the standards of the seafood industry	www.seafish.org +44 (0)131 558 3331
A website that unites all fish and chip shop operators in the UK	www.chippychat.co.uk
National Chip Week website	www.lovechips.co.uk
Trade magazine website	www.fry-online.co.uk
Food standards agency website	www.food.gov.uk
Holland's pies	www.hollandspies.co.uk
Pukka pies	www.pukkapies.co.uk
Wright pies	www.wrightpies.co.uk
Peters pies	www.petersfood.co.uk
Shire pies	www.shirefoods.com

RECOMMENDED SAUSAGE BRANDS

Tastybake	www.tasty-bake.co.uk
McWhinneys	www.mcwhinneyssausages.com
Blakemans	www.blakemans.co.uk
Pukka catering sausages	www.pukkapies.co.uk/product-range

BUSINESS SUPPORT CONTACTS

Federation of small businesses	www.fsb.org.uk
UK nation	www.uknation.co.uk

Business link	www.businesslink.gov.uk
Startups	www.startups.co.uk
New business	www.newbusiness.co.uk
Small business	www.smallbusiness.co.uk
My business	www.mybusiness.co.uk
The retail doctor	www.theretaildoctor.co.uk
Small business pro	www.smallbusinesspro.co.uk
Business gateway	www.bgateway.com
UK business forum	www.ukbusinessforums.co.uk
Growing your own business	www.growingyourownbusiness.co.uk
Business wings	www.businesswings.co.uk
Advice 4 businesses	www.advice4businesses.co.uk
BT get started	www.insight.bt.com
Clearly business	www.clearlybusiness.com
Cobweb	www.cobwebinfo.com

OTHER USEFUL CONTACTS

VAT HM revenue & customs	www.hmrc.gov.uk
National Insurance enquiries	0845 915 4655
Environment agency	08708 506 506
Health and safety website	www.hse.gov.uk
Newly self-employed helpline	0845 915 4515
New employer helpline	0845 60 70 143
National minimum wage helpline	0845 600 0678
Self assessment helpline	0845 900 0444

INDEX